...ent

The World

Temperance

The Devil

Death

The Hanged Man

Justice

The Hierophant

The Lovers

The Emperor

Priestess

The Empress

Confessions
of a
Tarot Reader

Confessions
of a
Tarot Reader

PRACTICAL ADVICE FROM THIS REALM AND BEYOND

JANE STERN

Guilford, Connecticut
An imprint of Globe Pequot Press

skirt!® is an attitude . . . spirited, independent, outspoken, serious, playful and irreverent, sometimes controversial, always passionate.

Text design: Sheryl P. Kober
Layout: Maggie Peterson
Project editor: Kristen Mellitt

Library of Congress Cataloging-in-Publication Data is available on file.

ISBN 978-1-59921-993-6

Printed in China

10 9 8 7 6 5 4 3 2 1

To the two queens,
Bunny and Joanne,
and my friend Diane

Contents

Contents

Welcome to Your Reading

You may be an old hand at knowing the ins and outs of the tarot deck or a frightened newbie curious but uncertain about what the cards will reveal. You may be a skeptic prepared to lie to me the entire hour to see if I can see through your bluff, or you may be at your wit's end, looking for any shred of hope in a dismal situation.

Before I even shuffle the deck or hand it to you to shuffle to infuse it with your energy, here is what I already know about you. You wouldn't be here unless you were at a crossroads in your life and having a hard time finding the correct path. Something has come up that you need hard answers to. A real tarot card reading is intrusive, and—as with psychotherapy—few people want their lives laid bare for fun. If you are looking for a party psychic or an old theatrical witch in a turban, you have come to the wrong place. I do not do parlor entertainment, nor do I want to scream to be heard over the band at your son's Bar Mitzvah. I will tell you what I see in the cards and I will not sugarcoat it, but neither will I be cruel.

I am compassionate and know how hard it is to implement change, and how brave you are to let me into your life as a helpmate.

As far as tarot readers go, I am an odd duck. I do not sit at a booth on the boardwalk, nor will you find me behind a neon sign in a storefront. I have a master's degree from Yale University and a well-established career as a writer. Yes, I am *that* Jane Stern, the expert on American road food, the volunteer EMT whose career inspired Kathy Bates to direct and play me in a movie about my life.

Why tarot cards? you may be wondering. The fact is that I grew up reading cards. My great-grandmother read cards and was a hands-on healer in Russia, where she rode town-to-town on horseback to cure the sick. In my family reading tarot cards was the sole territory of women. My mother had three brothers (who all became prominent psychoanalysts) and they in turn had daughters, but I was the only one who was the daughter of a daughter of a daughter, so I was introduced to tarot cards and my cousins were not. My mother was far from a peasant; likewise with me. I grew up on Sutton Place in New York City, and my mother was a concert pianist trained at Juilliard. Reading cards was folded into the daily routine of life and seemed not at all strange to me. It was just something we did along with ballet lessons, visits to the Central Park Zoo, and hot chocolate at Rumpelmayer's after ice-skating at Wollman Rink.

In my late teens I began reading cards for my friends. I used a deck of playing cards (old school) and did not switch to a tarot deck until I was in my twenties. I found reading cards easy as pie; I found telling my friends what I saw absolute hell.

How do you tell a smitten girl that her boyfriend is cheating on her or that her sister will soon grow very ill? If you were me back then, you would lie . . . and soon learn the hard way that truth is the essential component to being a tarot card reader. It is fun to see the radiant smile on a friend's face when you tell her how wonderful her boyfriend is, but it is awful when three weeks later she calls you in tears telling you that not only is he a bastard, but everything you said was wrong. If you are not ready to speak or hear the truth, don't have your cards read.

I always compare the way I read cards to a trip to the doctor (now, that's a fun prospect, isn't it?). But seriously, it is an apt analogy on many levels. Imagine if your cholesterol was through the roof, but the doctor did not want to upset you and ruin your day so he said it was fine. It wouldn't be very helpful in the long run. A good doctor won't scare you but will gently help you remedy what is wrong, which is the way I work.

Another way the medical model is useful is with new clients. They have obviously come to see me because something is troubling them. But in a test of my powers they will not tell me what is going on; they want me to psychically glean this information. Compare this with going to your doctor with a sore shoulder. You sit in his office, and he says, "What brings you in today?" You refuse to tell him. He spends the better part of an hour probing and poking as you sit smugly with your lips pursed, until eventually he touches your shoulder and you say, "Ouch." Would it not be easier and more cost-effective to just say "My shoulder hurts" and let him proceed with a cure? Please do not test me by asking me where you were born (unless you truly do not know), what the last four digits on your driver's license are, or the names of your last three cats. I am not a mind reader, I am a tarot card reader, so please let me do what I am really good at. Sometimes during a reading that goes along the *Prove it to me* line (men seem to like to take this tactic), I have to suppress a laugh, because sitting across from me is an otherwise savvy captain of industry paying me a rather large amount of money to tell him things he already knows. Is it really worth an hour of his time for me to tell him his cat's name is Miss Kitty?

At this point you may be wondering what the difference is between a psychic and a tarot card reader. I can only speak for myself, but from what I have seen over the years "psychics" claim they channel spirits—guides who make them talk in weird voices or go into trances. I am not taken over by another entity, I remain myself during a reading, and I let the tarot card layout explain to me why people are having their particular problems and what they should do about them. Maybe it is channeling the same energy but without the theatrics. Reading cards is like peeling an onion; I usually do seven or eight hands in a reading, and each hand reveals layers of information. I may be psychic or just wildly intuitive, but I seem to be able to pick up on details about my clients and the cast of characters in their lives (living and dead) easily.

One thing I am sure of is that tarot cards really work. They have been used as a method of personal discovery for centuries. They first appeared in the 1400s and were thought so potent they were immediately banned by the church. Some of the earliest decks from the fifteenth and sixteenth centuries (like the Visconti Modrone deck) now are housed at Yale's Beinecke Library. Sigmund Freud's colleague Carl Jung used the cards as symbols of what he called universal archetypes, believing they are the golden path into the psyche and blend common sense with mystical insights. I respect the power of the cards, and they have provided me with the rewards of insight.

Because the art of reading tarot cards is to illuminate the client's questions, the answers change depending on whom you are sitting across the table from. Obviously every person's layout (the order in which cards are placed on the table after they are shuffled) will be unlike that of any other person. Every client of mine or yours (and I use the term *client* rather loosely throughout the book, meaning the person you are reading for, be it a friend, a relative, or someone who is paying you a fee) will be wildly different from the next, even if on the surface they appear similar.

I remember once reading cards for a group of country-club ladies who at first glance could have been clones. They all wore matching pink-and-green Lilly Pulitzer shifts, all had the same streaked blond hair, and all had nicknames like Binky, Winky, and Muffy. When their cards hit the table, though, you could not have found six more different personalities grappling with six more disparate situations. Some of the ladies were happy, others miserable, some were sick, some healthy, some of their kids were high achievers, others candidates for juvenile hall. Do not ever be fooled by your client's facade, because it is just that: a screen on which she projects what she wants you to know about her. Your job is to look behind the screen—and this task varies greatly in difficulty. After some readings I am ready to pick out my wardrobe for my forthcoming Nobel Prize; other times I wonder who snuck into my bedroom at night and gave me a lobotomy with an ice pick. Every reading is unique, and much of it depends on the intangible chemistry between reader and client.

***

Confessions of a Tarot Reader is not a how-to book for would-be tarot card readers, but rather a summary of knowledge I have gleaned over my long career reading cards. This book is about how people unwittingly make poor decisions and find themselves in emotional (and occasionally physical) jeopardy. My insights and observations will show you the pitfalls of your actions—and, more important, the uncanny simplicity of finding the right answer—as well as how to recover from the cycle of hurtful habits.

It is important for you to know that I am what's referred to as a clean reader. I am not a witch, I do not dabble in the dark arts, and if ghosts appeared during my readings I would be out the door faster than you! But I have the ability to lift the veil between this world and the unseen world, and with this book so can you. Here you will see that the tarot deck is the best method for seeking answers from beyond the limited realm of our thought.

This book is filled with stories of clients I have worked with, and how they did or did not utilize the lessons learned. Some stories are funny (the client who greeted me at the door wearing a towel because he confused me with the appointment he made that day with a massage therapist), sad (the woman with four autistic children who was overwhelmed by her situation and needed help to move forward), and scary (counseling a client over the phone while her husband held a gun to her head). With this book you will learn from what other people did, and you will be able to chart your own progress to help you attain what you want in life.

The book is divided into twenty-two chapters, each ruled by one of the twenty-two Major Arcana cards in the full tarot deck of seventy-eight. The Major Arcana cards are the heavy hitters, known as the heart of the tarot, and they bear provocative titles like the Lovers, Death, the Wheel of Fortune, Strength, the Devil, the Tower, and the Fool. The Major Arcana cards deal directly with facets of our soul: the light, the dark, our dreams, fears, wishes, and determinations.

I truly hope that this book helps you gain insight. Imagine you are sitting across from me in my sunny blue-and-white living room in Connecticut with the birds chirping outside the window and the cherry tree in bloom. I have placed a cup of tea on the table for you, next to a box of Kleenex in case you need to wipe your eyes. I hand you the deck to shuffle, and we are off on a journey together.

A Note About the Cards

It doesn't much matter which tarot deck you refer to when using this book, but I have chosen to illustrate the twenty-two Major Arcana cards with one of the most unusual decks and a personal favorite, the spectacularly beautiful Bohemian Gothic Tarot designed by artists and tarot scholars Karen Mahony and Alex Ukolov, who run the Baba Studio in Prague, Czech Republic. The images are not as common as those in the Rider-Waite deck, which are ubiquitous when anyone discusses tarot cards. These you can see anytime you Google the words tarot card. I use the Rider-Waite cards when I lecture on tarot, and often when I read for my clients, but the Bohemian Gothic cards are such showstoppers I could not resist using them in this book.

If you are not used to seeing this deck, you may be a bit shocked by its rather spooky dark images, but that is intentional. Even the happy cards like the Sun, the Lovers, and the World have a less-than-cheerful look in this deck. The Bohemian Gothic deck links to the part of our personality that the psychoanalyst Carl Jung (whose name you will see

*throughout this text) calls our Shadow side, and these fasci-
nating images allow us to delve deeper into the links among
our conflicting emotions. So please don't get spooked by the
skulls and gargoyles and other creepy icons in these cards.
They hold the same meaning as all tarot card decks and will
lead you to learn more about your own life journey.*

*For more information on these wonderful cards and
related tarot items, visit www.babastudio.com.*

THE FOOL

THE FOOL

CARD NUMBER 0

Virtue, dear friend, needs no defense. The surest guard is innocence: None knew, till guilt created fear, what darts or poisoned arrows were.

—HORACE (65–8 BC)

Let me introduce you to the first Major Arcana card in the tarot deck: the Fool. The Fool is but one of twenty-two Major Arcana cards in the deck. *Major Arcana* is a fancy way of saying "big mysteries," and because this particular group of cards is the focus of this book, you will see this term often. For the rest of the journey through the twenty-one other cards, we will follow the Fool and see the trials and obstacles he must face.

Every one of the Major Arcana cards in contemporary decks has a number, and that number is consistent from one deck to the next. The Fool card is number zero. He represents the raw clay of humanity that the fates can mold depending on the choices he makes along the way. Zero is not really a number in the formal sense, but a symbol of nothing and everything, the beginning and the end, alpha and omega, and what better number for the Fool to be?

If you were to lay out all the Major Arcana cards in the deck in the order in which they are numbered, you would be able to see what lies ahead for the Fool. Will he fall from grace, or ascend in the highest manner? Will he be wise or stupid? Will he fail or conquer? The outcome is yet unknown. Why should we care? Because the Fool is all of us, and how he maneuvers through life mirrors our own journey. His choices are our choices, and the result equally personal. The Fool is you.

The Fool is all of us as we start out in life. We are guileless and happy. Everything is new and shiny and exciting. If you have ever watched a baby or toddler react to the world, you have a sense of the wonder apparent in the Fool. The Fool is wowed by life; he is at once awed and frightened. What we hope for him is that no matter what complications are thrown at him on his long journey, he is able to pick himself up when he stumbles and start again down the path. Personally the Fool card does not excite me the way some of the other Major Arcana cards do—you will see me slobbering over them later on in this book. I think of the Fool card as pulling the car out of the driveway. Is this the most exciting part of a long trip? No, but it is the beginning.

With that said, the tarot deck without the Fool tells no story. I do wish this card had a different name, because unless clients are conversant with tarot they often think when this card is pulled that I am calling them idiots. And who can blame them? I wouldn't want to be labeled a fool either. I often wish I could simply pick up a scissor and trim the words THE FOOL off the bottom of the card. No one would be the wiser, but people I read for might wonder why one card is an inch shorter than the rest. (I guess I could blame it on my dog.)

Some tarot enthusiasts argue that the alternative name for the Fool is the Joker and that he is a wild card. I do not agree; I find him neither wild nor Joker-like, but rather an unformed soul on his path to maturity and wisdom. Yes, he can act stupid or crazy, but that is just one aspect of the Fool's persona.

Fool is an old-fashioned term for an innocent being, a naive soul who bravely sets out to see what life is all about. In some decks his figure is shown against a bright blue sky, his knapsack is slung over his left shoulder, a yellow flower blooms in his palm, and his little dog frolics at his feet. What a lovely picture, except for one thing: He is about to fall off a pedestal suspended in midair. He does not see the imminent danger because he is gazing at the horizon. In our Bohemian Gothic deck, the Fool appears to be sleepwalking or mesmerized, and he is dancing out to the edge of an abutment that anyone (but him) can see will soon send him toppling into space.

The image of the Fool is as mysterious as it is painful, but then again so is life. At some point we all fall off the proverbial cliff, and most of us have the resilience to scramble back up and start our journey again. As the Fool card shows, running into trouble is not something we see coming; trouble sneaks up on us and ambushes us when we are least expecting it. Trouble does not ask us when a good time is to stir up a mess; in fact, trouble likes to throw a curveball at us just when we can least deal with it.

Unlike the Justice card that we will analyze later on, the Fool card is not about cause and effect. If the path the Fool was on had a sign saying WATCH OUT, YOU ARE ABOUT TO FALL!, then the Fool would be rather stupid and deserving of what he gets. But the Fool, like most of us, did not ask for or foresee calamity happening; it just does. At this early stage of the game, he moves forward on faith alone, not using his good sense to appreciate the danger ahead. For the rest of his journey, his character will be tested to see how he survives life (or doesn't).

Let me tell you about how the Fool card relates to two very different clients I've read for. Jack had nothing but a string of bad luck. Within the course of a year, he lost his wife to cancer, and he lost his job because of all the days he sat at her bedside and could not go to work. As a result of losing his job and incurring enormous medical bills, he fell behind in his mortgage payments, and to make matters worse he developed painful sciatica that hounded him day and night. The stress he was under turned his mild stutter into a major problem; when he was interviewed for a new job, he became so tongue-tied he could hardly speak.

Let's put Jack aside and take a look at Jill. She too had many losses in the past year. Her husband left her when he found out she was having an affair with her boss. Her boss fired her when his own wife found out about the affair, and then she fell behind in her mortgage payments. Always a heavy smoker, her stress increased her cigarette consumption, resulting in a hacking cough day and night. Nothing seemed to go right for her, her kids didn't respect her, and she was unmotivated to find another job because she'd been treated so "unfairly" in her last one.

Do you see where I am going with this? Jack was the Fool; Jill was not. Jack was the victim of the "shit happens" school of life. What happened to him was not a result of making bad choices. Although he was regularly brought to his knees with despair at the many facets of his problems, he managed to get up and keep going. The last time I read his cards, he was tentatively exploring dating again via the Internet, he was seeing a doctor about the sciatica and a speech therapist for the stuttering, and he was actively job hunting. He had asked for a sit-down with the mortgage department at his bank, and as it turned out the man he spoke with had also lost his wife recently and was very compassionate. Jack had also gone on three job interviews. When he told one interviewer that he'd lost his previous job because he wanted to be by his dying wife's bedside and would do it again, he could see in the interviewer's eyes that she thought he was a man of character.

Unlike Jack, Jill did nothing to help herself. She went to bars at night and found a handful of other losers who enjoyed complaining to one another about how unfair things were. She had no sense of cause and effect. Yes, her smoking made her cough, but she preferred to blame it on the ozone level. Her previous boss had lied to her and told her he was leaving his wife when he wasn't. According to Jill, the angry wife was a jealous bitch, and if she hadn't interfered Jill and the boss would still be between the sheets and she would've had the raise he'd promised her.

Jill was not the Fool card, although she was a perfect definition of a fool in the modern sense: a self-deluded jerk. She saw no reason to start over on the path of life because in her mind life was not fair to her. She did nothing wrong but ended up a victim; she took no responsibility for her actions, blaming everyone else; and she was unable to learn from her downfalls and move on.

When the cards are shuffled and hit the table, we will see if you are Jack or Jill. In my own life, as I'm sure you have in yours, I have been hit smack in the face with problems that I did not see coming. I wanted to go to bed and stay there for eternity. I wanted to picket with a LIFE'S UNFAIR sign. I groused and grumbled and bitched until I could not stand the sound of my own voice another moment. But what makes me a Jack instead of a Jill is that I did not give up. No matter how crappy I felt, I kept walking the path forward toward the light. One foot in front of another, one step at a time, and I found that the promise the universe holds out for us—that good things are ahead—is true. To walk the path of life, you do not need to be fleet-footed or nimble, you just need to ambulate ahead in the best way you can. You can strut, you can limp, you can crawl—just keep going!

To be grown-ups means assessing whether the people we meet along the path are beneficial or detrimental. The Fool meets a big cast of characters along his way through the tarot deck: Some are good and some are bad. He must take the positive things from the good ones and move on from the bad ones.

There is an image that never leaves my mind when I think of the Fool card. Flipping through the channels on my TV set one evening, I happened upon the Military Channel and a documentary about marines going through the Crucible, an especially rough boot camp. One of the challenges is very long hikes dressed in full combat gear with backpacks and rifles. These men and women are already exhausted from lack of sleep, being chewed out by the drill sergeants, and the accumulated stress of everything else they are made to do in this introduction to military life. After the first few miles, some soldiers fall by the wayside, unable to walk another step. If they refuse the help of their platoon buddies who in some cases literally carry the fallen ones across the finish line, they are drummed out of the corp. They will not become marines.

If you walk the path of life alone, you are setting yourself up to fail. Surround yourself with "platoon buddies" who will help you forward when you can't do it yourself. The wise marine knows he is not an army of one, and is not afraid to reach out for the helping hand. Of course doing this correctly is not self-serving. When the time comes and you are the one expected to hold out a helping hand, you must step up and do it too.

THE MAGICIAN

THE MAGICIAN

CARD NUMBER 1

Magic is believing in yourself. If you can do that, you make anything happen.

——JOHANN WOLFGANG VON GOETHE

Maybe it is just me, but I have always been confused why this card is the first one on the Fool's journey, and why he meets the Magician before the parental figures of the Emperor or the Empress.

The Fool is raw clay, about to be formed on his long journey through the twenty-one other Major Arcana cards. On this journey he will find beauty and terror, joy and misery, the end and the beginning. Does he really need to meet David Copperfield first?

I am kidding (a bit), because the Magician card has taken quite a beating in modern times. When the tarot deck first came to popularity five centuries ago, a magician was an important figure and not a Las Vegas show act. Magicians, wizards, magi, and witches were feared and respected for their otherworldly powers. There were no Penns or Tellers around deconstructing how a trick worked, no mail-order magic books for the do-it-yourself types. If an intense-looking man in a cape made smoke rise from a goblet it was serious stuff, and you paid attention to him.

The key to this card lies in the objects on the table in front of the Magician. Think of this card as a recipe and the Magician as Julia Child. When a celebrity chef shows you how to cook something, she has the ingredients already laid out on the table. "Here is the butter, here is the salt, and here is the chicken," she will explain. In fact there are a hundred ways to combine those ingredients to make a hundred different dishes, but the chef has decided which combination it will be. The Magician card is about combining the raw ingredients of life in many different ways. Does the Magician (fate) decide? Or do you (the Fool)? I think it is the partnership between these two elements that makes for a good outcome.

The Magician has spread out all the ingredients of life in front of him and is telling the Fool that it is his choice to mix and match them in any way he wishes. Freedom of choice is a large part of what this card signifies, making the Magician one of the most important cards relating to the life force of creativity. Life, for any of us, comes down to the art of deciding what goes with what, editing our choices, redoing and revamping ideas until it feels right. We will like a person at first, and then maybe later we decide we don't. A job looks promising, but soon turns into a dead end. Why did you never notice that girl in the corner by herself before? Why on earth did you dye your hair red? The Magician card tries to teach us that figuring out the best way to get along in life is up to *us*.

This card has both good and bad meanings, depending on whether it's dealt right-side up or reversed. Many of the cards are optimistic turned one way and bad turned the other. Right-side up the Magician represents charm, diplomacy, confidence, and mastery. But in addition to these positive virtues, it can foretell willfulness and disaster befalling the client. Reversed it can refer to doctors and medical healing but also to craziness and shame. Why is this card so complicated? Probably because that's how life itself is, and the Magician is getting the Fool ready for the house of mirrors he is about to enter, where nothing will be as it seems.

At this point in his journey, the Fool is very naive and hopeful. What better audience for a slick magician? The Swiss psychoanalyst Carl G. Jung knew that magic and miracles are closely related as types of mystical experience. He thought they had one element in common: "an attitude of hopeful expectancy on the part of the participants." Based on tests of extrasensory perception, Jung classed people as either doubters or hopefuls. The hopefuls had a higher score of precognition for a hidden word on the back of a card than the doubters. The bottom line is that someone anticipating a miracle is more likely to get it than a naysayer. Magic apparently does not happen to cynics.

There are some clients whom I find almost impossible to work with. Fortunately it doesn't happen often, but when it does it leaves me with a profound sense of sadness. David was such a fellow. He was a police detective by trade and for fun he read forensics books. Clearly this was a man who liked proof and not speculation, so why did he come to me for a reading to begin with? His girlfriend had given him a gift of a tarot reading (I am sure he would have much preferred a thermal coffee mug).

What David did not know about me is that—for a mystical sort—I too am a bit of a cynic. In a classroom or a lecture on something otherworldly, I will be the one rolling her eyes or scribbling *bullshit* in the margins of my notebook. This may be an outgrowth of hearing one too many stories from clients of devious practices used by people from whom they sought help. Like David, I do not take things at face value.

This was David's first (and only) tarot reading with me. In this case he was the embodiment of the Fool (a word I wouldn't dare say out loud to him for fear he might pistol-whip me). But unlike the happy-go-lucky Fool, his questions were guarded, almost to the point of my not understanding what he wanted to know, but I persevered. As I remember it, the Magician was very active in David's reading, and although I had seen this card a million times before I had never focused so clearly on the implements laid out on his table. The Magician's tools were as well chosen as the ones David used in a police investigation. Each tool was designed to dig deeper for clues and answers. Suddenly the card seemed methodical and not magical, a good beginning for finding common ground with this man.

We didn't get very far at all. David was a doubter of such magnitude that I could not get him even for one moment to suspend disbelief and see if we could move together into uncharted waters. I knew I had lost him at the beginning when he asked me how the cards worked and I truthfully said I didn't know and that they were a mystery even to me. I felt the way a priest must feel when cornered by an atheist who demands proof of God's existence. Telling someone like this to go on faith is not enough. If my tarot cards were like magic tricks, I could have taken David behind the scenes and shown him the secrets, but the cards are not so literal, and sadly I was not able to reach a mutually comfortable meeting ground with him. The reading was a wash. What made this especially frustrating for me was that intuitively I felt that the cards had much to say to David. Asking someone to take things on faith and to trust you is a tall order and not something everyone feels comfortable with.

I am far from being Aesop or one of the Brothers Grimm, but I will tell you a little fable of my own called The Celestine Garbage Can. My dear friend Bunny spends much of our time together showing me her forearms and exclaiming that her hair is again standing on end. Bunny is very much in touch with things of another realm, she knows when people are going to die (although she has an admitted problem of always being one day ahead of their demise), and she is conversant with the spiritual. Bunny is also a great fan of books like *The Celestine Prophecy,* a best-selling novel that offers a key to ancient wisdom and the power of synchronicity. When Bunny gets excited about something, she talks about it non-stop and very fast, so as we pulled into the parking lot of Bed Bath & Beyond one day, she was confusing me with talk about what she was looking for (a particular type of wastebasket) mixed up with discussion of the novel. We were wheeling our carts around when she stopped dead in her tracks. She showed me her arm—and yes, the hair was standing on end. "I can't believe it," she stammered. "I visualized it and there it is . . . the perfect garbage can . . . it is the Celestine Garbage Can." She cried with joy.

The reason I'm bringing this rather silly story into the mix is that the Magician card is a very powerful ally of synchronicity. Synchronicity is a common and strange phenomenon: You are thinking of someone and suddenly spot her last name painted on a semitruck in front of you, or you see a pair of red shoes like your childhood best friend used to wear and out of the blue she calls to say hi. Is synchronicity magic? Perhaps it is. Jung explained it as a "kind of coincidence between internal states and external events." We cannot call it forth at will, it just happens, and when it does it always comes as a surprise, along with a *Twilight Zone* chill and, in Bunny's case, arm hair standing on end.

Our inner magician is not going to reveal all his tricks to us; he wants to grab our full attention with the big payoff when he pulls the proverbial rabbit out of the hat. Who has not wrestled with a problem, sitting restlessly in a chair, pondering every possible aspect of the situation—and still not moving one inch closer to an answer? Then in the morning you are making coffee or letting the dog out and like a bolt from the blue comes your answer. It all falls together like a jigsaw puzzle completed. Sometimes the solution is obvious and sometimes unique, but the veil that keeps you from it lifts on its own time frame, not yours. When this happens, think of the Magician, because he is in charge of things being revealed.

———•———

You may get the impression that the Magician card and I are close friends. In truth he rarely shows up in my readings. My cards are to me very real entities. They can be stubborn or silly or lazy. I used to take riding lessons, and my cards often remind me of the horses that are rented by the hour. I have never seen a horse wearing a wristwatch, but when the hour is up the horse will stop trotting around the ring and stand at the gate waiting for you to dismount. Because my readings are one hour, my cards automatically shut down at the end of this time frame. Even when I want to do a longer reading, it is up to the goodwill of the cards to allow the extension; sometimes they do and sometimes they don't. How do I know when they shut down? When the layout is tarot gibberish and there is no connection from one card to the next. The cards have hung up an Out to Lunch sign and will return only when the next client arrives. As living things, my decks have many moods that I can sense. Often they are slow to get into the reading; sometimes they really do not like the client, and it's a struggle to get them to focus. You may be thinking that I am projecting my feelings into the cards, but I do not agree. Many times I am at odds with the cards, and that leaves me little doubt that they have a will and mind of their own.

THE HIGH PRIESTESS

THE HIGH PRIESTESS

CARD NUMBER 2

The mystical life is the centre of all that I do and all that I think and all that I write . . .

—WILLIAM BUTLER YEATS

One of the most common questions I get from clients is how they might tap into their hidden potential. Many of us feel that there is some sort of invisible wall or curtain blocking the view of the path we should be on. The tarot card known as the High Priestess concerns this covert and mysterious part of life, and when used correctly she can light the way.

The High Priestess's depiction is intriguing: A beautiful woman sits between two pillars, one black and one white. She stares right at you and appears to see through to your very soul.

As noted, on the Fool's journey he meets the Magician and the High Priestess before he meets the parental figures of the Emperor and Empress. The Magician and High Priestess are more elemental, concerning themselves with the intangible, mysterious forces that shape us and then reside forever in our deep unconscious, where we may or may not be in touch with them. The High Priestess is very much concerned with personality balance in a yin–yang sort of way. If the Magician is about active power, the High Priestess is about the more mysterious things that shape our internal decision making. She is the night to the Magician's day; she is mysterious when he is blunt. Personally I find her the more interesting of the pair.

Clearly, if you are in search of answers this lady is your first stop. She holds the keys to the mind and knows what is behind the curtain. She is so seductive as a guide through the veils that many tarot readers choose her as the one card in the deck that symbolizes them. Mine (and I suspect I share it with twelve million other mysterious dark-haired tarot-reading ladies) is also the High Priestess.

Carl G. Jung used the tarot deck in his work, and recognized the High Priestess as the embodiment of what he called the Shadow. The Shadow is one of the archetypes that Jung felt all human beings share no matter their culture, sex, or age, and in this case it is symbolic of all the mysteries that lie below the surface of every man and woman's unconscious mind. Some people call the Shadow the "dark side" (which sounds unnecessarily ominous); others call it the "repressed" part of our personalities that we are out of touch with. Either way, the Shadow is in charge of all the private, troubling things that most of us know about ourselves but work very hard to make sure no one else sees— that is, if we are relatively emotionally healthy. The people who get in serious trouble with their Shadow sides are those who refuse to see and categorically deny being anything but the adorable, loving, and caring people they project to the world. I can assure you even Mother Teresa had a dark side, even if it was only grumbling to herself that her feet hurt at the end of the day.

I had a client I will call Rachel who was in a battle with her Shadow side. She was the mother of a young woman who was about to be married. Rachel (on the surface) was the most attentive, kind, and self-sacrificing woman on the face of the earth. She sewed her daughter's elegant bridal dress by hand, she was planning to bake the elaborate wedding cake herself, and she spent half her life's savings to send her daughter and new son-in-law on a round-the-world cruise. The problem that arose in our reading was that every time Rachel meant to say the word "wedding" she accidentally said "funeral." She didn't hear herself say this, and when I called her attention to this slip of the tongue she acted like I was making things up.

Poor Rachel exhausted herself by acting the part of the perfect mother although she had a deep dislike for her new son-in-law and felt her daughter was making a mockery of everything Rachel stood for by marrying him. She covered up this poisonous animosity by putting on an enormous show of love and concern for the betrothed couple, when in fact if a brick fell from the sky and killed the bridegroom Rachel would have (subconsciously) done a wild jig of happiness. Not even to herself could she admit her dark feelings.

Being honest with ourselves is possibly the hardest task any of us can take on. It requires extreme self-examination and honesty, and recasting the self in another persona. Many people simply cannot do this hard work. How they think the world sees them is so important that even within the privacy of their own minds, they can't admit to being flawed. You will be able to identify these poor souls because while on the surface they seem like they have it all together, they radiate a deep sense of shame. They are always making up reasons why other people get ahead in life and they don't. They blame others for their own lack of success because they believe they are perfect in every way. If they fail, it is never their fault but a result of the fact that people do not understand them. They are finger pointers who have a long list of excuses why they can't get ahead in life. With this attitude they have sealed their own fates and thrown away the key.

When I think back to Rachel, I always think of the old adage "You can lead a horse to water but you can't make him drink." Only people who are open to accepting that they are not in sync with their inner feelings will ever get beyond the barrier they're up against and move on. You'll never get rid of your Shadow side, but in a healthy life you can acknowledge the existence of your less-than-delightful inner thoughts and incorporate them as a whole in your personality. The Shadow side serves a purpose. Marion Woodman, one of Jung's disciples, pointed out that "We have day time and night time. Which one of us would want no night time? Imagine the stress of always having to be 'on,' to be cheerful and perky and never take off your stage make-up. That truly would be hellish."

Long ago I learned that to challenge a client's Shadow statements means walking on thin ice. Pointing out that someone's snarky jibes are more mean than funny, I get back "You have no sense of humor"; if a client of mine thinks commenting cruelly on other people's weight, wardrobe, or hairdo is doing any kind of service, rather than being a crappy way to behave, I will point this out. Of course I am often subject to a barrage of great denial and much flapdoodle that I am misreading their actions.

When I read cards, I use the High Priestess in a few different ways. If you, like me, choose the High Priestess as your personal card, you can use its appearance in a reading as a sign to yourself that you are on the right path. It is my "Good Housekeeping Seal of Approval," telling me that I am getting an accurate take on my client. But I don't get so carried away that I forget she can also be a real pain in the ass, and one of the most frustrating cards to deal with.

Let me explain. I think we can divide the world into two sets of people: those who love to analyze things, and those who run screaming from insights as if they were in a burning house. I am squarely in the first group. I am a Scorpio, the "detective" of the zodiac, and I am from a family of shrinks whose business was unearthing endless insights from their patients' subconscious. Give me someone difficult to figure out, and I am in hog heaven.

Because I am pretty good at what I do (even without cards I have the talent to see someone's persona rather clearly), it can be seductive to just bark out what I see and expect my client to "get it." It doesn't work that way. A tarot reader is comparable to an archaeologist on a dig. Have you seen one with a feather, gently working her way through layers of dust? Sure, she could use a shovel and yank out the ancient bones or pottery shards, but she would probably destroy the find in the process. Same with working with clients: Go gently and slowly or you can destroy them.

You can't blurt out things like "Of course you feel that way, it is obvious you are gay"; or "Don't you know that you act like an obnoxious snob?" because the Shadow side of the client will reach across the table, smack you upside your head, and shut down. Easy does it.

If you read for others, or yourself, either for fun or in all seriousness, even making a little progress in identifying the Shadow side is a huge step toward self-actualization. To uncover and understand the blind spots in your own persona is a major accomplishment. What you have going for you is that nature loves balance, and being in tune with both sides of your personality is where nature wants you to go. If you are out of whack, it is because you are making it so.

Carl Jung sums up why we must do this balancing work: "Everyone carries a shadow, and the less it is embodied in the individual's conscious life the blacker and denser it is. At all counts, it forms an unconscious snag, thwarting our most well meaning intentions."

In other words (mine not Jung's), get real and get out of your own way.

Are there people without a Shadow side? Yes, but they are a world unto themselves. I am not talking about those self-styled sphinxes who will not let you pry anything from them at all. No, I am referring to a whole other kettle of fish.

Many years ago I had a client who taught me a thing or two about hidden mysteries and balancing the Shadow side with the light. She was a talented musician, a violinist at the Yale School of Music. Originally from Iowa, she had the clean-edged good looks of the former farm girl she was. She was a lovely presence and people naturally gravitated toward her—but then much to her dismay quickly ran the other way. She could not get a second date, her teachers gave her the minimal amount of time they could, and she had trouble getting a roommate to share her large and well-situated apartment.

We started by shuffling the deck of cards, and I laid them out. The young woman sitting across from me appeared utterly disconnected from her cards. In fact her cards seemed disconnected from one another. It was as if I'd just thrown them up at the ceiling and let them fall down at random. Because the job of a tarot reader is to use the cards to tell a story, to form a pattern that will provide answers, this was not helpful.

As I almost always do when I sit down for the first time with a client, I asked her to name three major issues going on in her life. She brightly answered, "School, men, and getting a roommate." Okay, so far, so good. Then I began to ask questions. "Tell me about the problems you are having at school." "I don't know what to tell you," she said, so I jumped over to men. "I really do not know what to tell you," she said again, offering me nothing. "The roommate problem?" I queried. "I don't know," she said flatly. After this glorious start I reshuffled the cards, and again the cards told no story; they were a scramble of meaningless chaos.

I poked and I prodded and I flipped questions every possible way, to no avail. Neither cards nor client would reveal anything at all, although she seemed not at all covert but as sunny and two-dimensional as a cardboard cutout of a pretty girl.

I saw her three times, and at the end of the third session we both realized we were going nowhere and parted company. For years I was bothered that I could find not a shred of material to understand her. I did not get the answer until about ten years later, when her image turned up on the local television station news show. She had been charged with a rather heinous crime, and the Yale community was abuzz over her actions. I must have heard a dozen times that she was "sociopathic."

Sociopaths can be charming and talented and very bright, but they are missing a great big hunk of their internal personalities. I learned that when interacting with a sociopath, many "normal" people sense a profound emptiness in this shell of a person and instinctively run away, even if they do not know why they are turned off. In retrospect I think this is what was underlying all three of the issues she brought to me: She projected nothing. Lights on, nobody home.

Now, please do not think that I am saying that every private person is a sociopath. Many people are guarded for a variety of reasons, both good and bad. Most of us prefer to keep our "constructed" personality intact as a shield to protect the vulnerable, painful part of our unprotected egos within. If you're a good tarot card reader, you can work well with very private people, assuming that they come to trust you over time and you show them a sensitivity that acknowledges how difficult they find it to open up. But you cannot read cards for facades of human beings who have nothing below the surface but thin air. I still can't say that I understand what did or did not go on in this client's head, but I do know that she never paid me for the card readings, and that she stole a pair of earrings from a side table when I went into the kitchen to get her a glass of water. Years later I feel very sorry for her (although I wish I had my earrings back). Imagine being a person who is only a surface?

So if you are a card-carrying sociopath and reading this book, I absolve you of searching for your inner being. If you aren't, get to work and explore your soul so you can move on in life and be productive and happy. It is hard work to explore your inner realms, but worth all the effort you spend on it.

THE EMPRESS

THE EMPRESS

CARD NUMBER 3

The formative period for building character for eternity is in the nursery. The mother is queen of that realm and sways a scepter more potent than that of kings or priests.
                                                    —AUTHOR UNKNOWN

Is there any word in any language more emotionally powerful than *mother*? Mothers are sanctified or damned; they bring tears to the eyes of children who love them and tears to the eyes of those who do not. Children, siblings, and husbands are optional; mothers are not. Everyone has one (even if you were conceived in a test tube), and how she nurtured or neglected you will be with you for the rest of your life.

The Empress card in the tarot deck is first and foremost a symbol of motherhood. Right-side up the Empress is bountiful, fertile, radiating health and sensuality. She is the card of all feminine power, beauty, comfort, and abundance.

The Empress card is the third Major Arcana card, and the Fool meets her very early on in his journey through life. This makes perfect sense, because mothers are not people we hook up with later; they are the hands that mold the clay that is us.

When I lecture on the tarot and speak about the Empress card, I show two slides to give people an idea of the vastly different personas of motherhood. First I show our modern goddess of motherhood: Heidi Klum, hugely pregnant and glowing with life, health, and happiness. Then I show a slide of Faye Dunaway in the movie *Mommy Dearest* portraying Joan Crawford with her adopted daughter Christina, age six. Joan is overly made up, her smile a rictus grin, her lips a clownish slash of red lipstick. She and her little daughter wear matching girlie-girl outfits. She is suffocating, smothering, and dangerous. I do not need to explain beyond this slide what the Empress reversed is about.

The Empress card has more mythic baggage than many of the other Major Arcana cards. Her depiction in the Bohemian Gothic Tarot deck is terrifying to me. She sits in the lap of bourgeois luxury with her child, but there is something terribly off kilter and monstrous about the picture. Most other decks paint a more benign picture of the Empress, as a beautiful woman, fertile and gracious. I like the Bohemian card because it perfectly exemplifies the dual nature of the goddess Persephone, daughter of the mighty Zeus and his formidable wife, Demeter, on whom the card is based. In her myth Persephone is seduced by Hades, god of the underworld, and brought below to his fiery realm.

Demeter vented her maternal anger at her daughter's kidnapping by ignoring the growing of plants, which was her earthly task. Instead she wandered the earth looking for her lost child. When the crops did not grow, both people and animals began to die of starvation. Distraught, Demeter asked Zeus to meet with Hades and negotiate Persephone's return. They did meet, but when Hades and Zeus could not reach a compromise, the almighty Zeus simply declared that since Persephone had not partaken of anything from Hades's garden, their marriage was null and void.

Seeming to acquiesce to Zeus, Hades bade farewell to Persephone, giving her a luscious pomegranate as a going-away gift. Like Eve with the forbidden apple in the Garden of Eden, Persephone took a bite; this act made her marriage to Hades forever binding. Having tasted the pomegranate, Persephone from that point forward divided her time—six months in fiery Hell and the other half of the year with Zeus and Demeter in the lush realm above. Therefore, the once ever-blooming garden of Demeter was allowed to bloom for only half of the year, when Persephone returned to her earthly home. As the myth states: When Persephone appears in the spring, plants blossom; when she leaves after the last harvest and returns to hell, everything dies.

Why are this strange myth and the Empress tarot card intertwined? The short answer is that motherhood is a very complicated affair, all tangled up in self-sacrifice, seduction, power plays, greed, the purest kind of love, and hell on earth. Like all mothers and daughters, Demeter and Persephone walked a hard path. In a way their relationship is as modern as an episode of Dr. Phil. I imagine them in their flowing gowns sitting on his stage arguing thusly:

DEMETER: I told you a million times that Hades was no good.

PERSEPHONE: You're not the boss of me.

DEMETER: Now look what you've done, you could have said no to the pomegranate.

PERSEPHONE: I was hungry, you're always telling me to eat something healthy, and when I do it turns into another thing for you to bitch about.

DEMETER: It is always something with you, you never think about what's best for the family.

DR. PHIL: After the commercial break we'll be joined onstage by Persephone's boyfriend Hades and her father Zeus. I guarantee you that this is a confrontation you do not want to miss! Stay tuned.

———•———

Throughout the centuries there have been other interpretations of the Empress card. Some say she is the Virgin Mary, others a *refugium peccatorum* (which sounds like a great Italian cheese but is a Latin term referring to a universal symbol of womanly fecundity). As various tarot decks go in and out of popularity, so does the image of the Empress. Some show her as a nice suburban mom, rather like Betty Crocker; for others she is a flat-out sexpot; and in the Rider-Waite deck she resembles a 1970s hippie chick with her long gauzy dress, blond curly hair, and bare feet.

The Empress is a card of fertility, joyfulness, and beauty—but she is also about compromise, which is what much of motherhood comes down to. Unless you are an in-home dictator like Joan Crawford, you must learn to take a little and give a little with your children, hope for the best, and be prepared to ride out the worst. It is almost guaranteed that they will refuse to marry the people you choose for them, get jobs you think are stupid, live in a ridiculous place—and then, just as you have run out of things to nag them about, they will return to the nest age thirty or older (possibly with babies of their own) and expect you to take care of them for the rest of their lives. Okay, some kids do grow up as planned but honestly most don't, and that is why the beautiful and troublesome daughter Persephone is shown on the Empress card and not her long-suffering mother, Demeter.

To get an honest take on new clients, I will occasionally pull a switcheroo. Instead of explaining things to them, I will lay out a hand of cards and ask them to tell me a story based on what they see in the cards. I do this only with clients unfamiliar with the tarot deck, so they do not have any preconceived notions. As with a Rorschach test, they come up with some strange and interesting insights. For one thing, rarely is the Empress card identified as a mother figure. She is seen as a rather vain prom queen type. When I point out that she is often used to represent motherhood, I usually get one of two replies. The first is, "Yes, I have seen my mother all dolled up like that and acting like a queen." The other is, "My mother doesn't look anything like that. She is an old lady, and all she does is sit around and worry."

Are any of us happy with our mothers? Yes, many are. But the very word is enough to open the floodgates of difficult memories. Once I identify this card as a "mother" card, it is often impossible for my clients to move beyond it as anything else. The Empress intrudes on the reading, taking up way too much airspace. As a reader the real difficulty comes when the Empress card presents itself as a metaphor for a new endeavor that needs nurturing, and is not literally about one's mother. When I was young and new at reading cards, I would talk myself in circles explaining the metaphor of the Empress, explaining how an idea is like the spark of gestation, how it slowly grows like a pregnancy, and then once the idea comes to fruition it still needs to be shaped and monitored. Eventually I came to realize that no one was listening to my blather. No one cared about mother metaphors, they wanted to talk about their real mothers, good, bad, and indifferent.

———— ·•· ————

I have two clients whom I will call Leslie and Jan. I find their stories revealing. Leslie is everyone's image of what a good mother should be. Miraculously she never fails to appear at any of the events in her four kids' busy lives. Be it soccer, cheerleading, riding lessons, or gymnastics, she is omnipresent and cheering like mad from the sidelines. Leslie bakes the best brownies for the PTA bake sale. She gives the most thoughtful presents to her kids' teachers at Christmas, and she practically single-handedly supports the local orthodontist. What people would never guess is that she hates being a mother. Her body is there at her kids' events, but her mind is a million miles away, probably thinking about the next time she can steal away to see her lover.

Leslie has dinner on the table for her husband and kids every night at 6:00 p.m. She cooks from scratch, never resorting to fast food. If they paid closer attention, her family might notice that she never sits at the table with them; instead she is always buzzing around the kitchen or straightening something up. At night she does not talk to her husband; she is busy sewing badges on her son's Cub Scout uniform or frosting cupcakes. What I know is that sooner or later, she will snap. She will simply collapse upon herself like a house of cards. When she cannot keep up the sham another moment, people in and out of her family will be stunned. Leslie is what I refer to as a "balloon person"—she gets bigger and shinier with each task she completes, and then with one breath too many she pops and disappears. Who will help put her back together? It is hard to say because basically no one really knows her true self.

My client Jan is a different story. No one would call her mother of the year. Her kids go to school with mismatched socks and unironed shirts; her husband often comes home after work to find a bucket of fried chicken with a funny note saying EAT ME Scotch-taped to it. The house is somewhat of a mess too: half-finished art projects, piles of library books, a well-loved but shedding dog, and cartoons pinned to the fridge. While Jan would never challenge Martha Stewart in the homemaking department, she is one of the best mothers I know. I have sat at her dinner table watching her whole family passionately arguing the merits of a recent movie. One of the kids is crazy for astronomy, while another likes to see how car engines work. They are bright and happy and the whole family has fun together, fun that doesn't mean a vacation to Disney World or lots of new designer clothes. The members of Jan's family truly enjoy one another's company, and it shows.

Motherhood is a very complicated affair if you don't like being a mother. If you do, it flows like a river. The question you must ask yourself in every situation is obvious: Is it right for the family as well as for me? The way the world sees your family is less important than the way you know it really is. This is one reason why the movie *Mommy Dearest* was so chilling: It depicted a relationship that was all facade and falseness, imitation of life at its cruelest.

There is one final aspect of this card that bears attention: the passing of time. Just as Persephone's actions caused there to be fruitful seasons and fallow seasons, the Empress card can be a warning that a client may not be using her time wisely. If I hear one thing over and over again from modern mothers, it is that there are not enough hours in the day. I also see way too many stressed-out mothers who take on more than anyone can reasonably do, and schedule their kids like mini executives with not a moment to spare. I am waiting for the day I hear a school-aged kid tell his friend, "Have your people call my people, and we will set up a date."

I will leave you with one final story that may be funny or tragic; I still can't decide. I was doing a reading for a mother who wanted her son to go to Yale. She had heard that I'd gone to college there, and knew I was an established writer with many books published. She seemed quite uninterested in her tarot reading, and finally came to the meat of why she was seeing me. "I would like you to write my son's essay in his application to Yale." I wondered if I had heard her correctly and stuttered something naive like, "Isn't he supposed to write it himself?" She snorted and rolled her eyes at me as if I had just crawled out of a cave somewhere in the hinterlands. She went on to explain the very serious and competitive business of getting into a top college, and how having a professional "shape" your essay was a common practice. I was shocked. I was even more shocked when the sum of money this well-heeled lady offered me matched the advance I had received for my latest book. There are things I have done in my life that I am not proud of, but this was not to be one of them. I turned the offer down, got another snort and eye roll, and she was on her way out the door.

I am sure this mother found someone else to "shape" the essay, and very possibly the boy got into Yale, but at what emotional cost? Maybe she was prepared to pave the way for him his whole life and had the resources to do it. Maybe it was less about him and more about her bragging rights at the country club. I would love to be a fly on the wall thirty years hence when the boy (now a confused middle-aged man) is stretched out on the shrink's couch trying to figure out why he always feels like a fraud.

THE EMPEROR

THE EMPEROR

CARD NUMBER 4

I have tasted command and can no longer give it up.
—NAPOLEON BONAPARTE

Hello, Big Daddy! The Fool meets the Emperor very early on in his journey and is wildly impressed—and why not? The Fool is a young whippersnapper and the Emperor is a majestic figure sitting high on his golden throne. All of us have met the Emperor at some point in our lives. He may be a father, a professor, a boss, a religious leader, a commanding officer, or any masculine figure who is large and in charge. The Fool feels both in awe of him and protected by him. As we (or the Fool) go through our lives, it is likely we will not have this exalted feeling again in someone's presence. We learn that all leaders have feet of clay, but for now the Emperor seems flawless and in utter command.

When I lecture on tarot, I show slides to illustrate my talking points. When I search for slides that exemplify the Emperor, I am always struck by how many there are to choose from. The figure of a ruler on a throne is a symbol that dates back to earliest civilizations. Egyptians, Greeks, and other ancient class-bound societies all had a king. The symbolism of this figurehead is everywhere. Some headmen are benevolent and some are tyrants.

Let me tell you about two clients I have, one a boss, and the other an underling in a big corporation. The boss is a wonderful person. Wallace treats his employees like a family; he knows their names and their family situations. His employees know they can go to him with a problem and he will help solve it. Few people are ever fired or leave their jobs with Wallace's company. His turnover rate is so low that he has a long list of applicants who would love to fill any vacant positions. His production capacity is also very high, because people who work for him feel valued and care about what they do at work.

Then there is Mitch. Mitch is the proverbial cog in the wheel of some big faceless corporation. For the first year he worked there, people called him by the name of the last guy who sat at his desk; it seemed too much trouble to learn his name. Once he came for a reading and I noticed that the lapels of his sports jacket looked odd. "What is that on your jacket?" I asked. "Spit," he replied. His company had bosses on top of bosses, each section answering to higher-ups. Mitch was constantly being yelled at by his section boss—yelled at with such venom that the boss could not control his saliva flow. "You are not living up to our expectations," the boss yelled at Mitch, who wanted to reach back to the fifth grade when you could say "Say it, don't spray it" to such creeps. The anger that his higher-up showed is indicative of the organization. It is run by fear, and people feel under the gun at all times. Mitch didn't stay at the job long. Wallace on the other hand is running out of twenty-five-year pins and other awards to honor his employees.

Without realizing it Wallace was acting in the way of kings of old—the good kings, that is. He had established an order within his business where his court felt directly connected with him. If the king was happy, his subjects were happy; if the king was troubled, so were they. Mitch on the other hand had no such emotional investment in his job. He had never seen or met the head of the corporation, and the concept of his being a valued employee was just that, a concept.

In almost every tarot deck, the Emperor is sitting in a throne, a golden crown on his head and a scepter in his hand. He looks positively glued to the chair; it would be hard to imagine him ever standing up. The Emperor card is ruled by the astrological sign of Aries, and Aries people are known for an almost uncanny ability to act on instinct instead of insight. They like to be first, they like to be noticed and respected, and when pushed too hard they can become warriors. It takes them a minute or two to remember that they are not the boss of everyone and everything.

The warrior side of the Emperor card cuts two ways in the tarot deck. If you live in a country under attack, you want a very strong ruler. If you have such a person in charge, you will be safe; if the nation is harmed, it will be defended. The Emperor card dealt right-side up signifies a powerful force for protection. You will be taken care of under his mantle. The Emperor reversed is another story. The Emperor turned either way will not shy away from confrontation, but when the card is reversed in a reading it is a warning sign to the client that whomever he thinks will protect him is not up to the job. The Emperor card reversed is like being in a bar where some big mouth insults the Hell's Angels crowd—and as they prepare to defend their turf the big mouth disappears. You are left with a dozen bikers coming at you.

In numerology the Emperor card is number four, and four is a big deal in the realm of tarot. Think of all the defining things that come in fours: the four seasons, the four winds, the Four Horsemen of the Apocalypse, the four phases of the moon, the four elements (air, water, earth, and fire), the four points of the compass . . . the list is long, and this is just a sampling. Because the number four is so relevant in how we define and classify things, it is a perfect number for the Emperor: If all is well with him, all is well with us. Everything is in place and accounted for.

When a client draws the Emperor card, I begin with the obvious questions. What is his relationship with his father? What is his boss at work like? How do his children or employees see him? Was his own father brutal, distant, loving, or absent? If an actual father figure does not reveal a direction for the cards to go in, then I go to the second level, which is to discuss mastery. The Emperor card is often a marker of someone striving to accomplish a task—perhaps excelling at a discipline such as karate, archery, woodworking, bridge, or becoming fluent in a language. When the card is dealt reversed, it often means the person I am reading for has hit a wall in this quest and is not progressing. Another aspect this card indicates is a struggle for power within a relationship. Although it is trendy to speak of being equal partners, most relationships find one person being more dynamic then the other. Whoever is the more dominant figure is symbolized by the Emperor, be this a male or a female.

My clients Alan Senior and Alan Junior are good examples. Alan Senior is the founder and CEO of a business so vast that all of you would know the name instantly. They are both nice men, intelligent and generous, but that's where the similarity ends. Alan Junior inherited the family business from his father, who in turn was put in charge when his father retired. Because the firm is such an integral part of the family identity, it was simply assumed that the mantle of leadership would be passed down through the generations.

When I read for Alan Senior, the Emperor card is very active. It's almost always dealt right-side up and often in the center. Being the head of this company is Alan Senior's dream come true. As a little boy he loved nothing better than to go to his father's grand office on the top of a skyscraper and watch him work. Laughingly he told me that his favorite toy was not a train or a stuffed animal but an old briefcase his father gave him when he bought himself a new one.

When I read for Alan Junior, the Emperor card also came up often, but always reversed. After months of reading for Junior, who verbally was the company's biggest cheerleader and never failed to mention the cachet that his last name held in society, it became clear that the last thing he wanted to do was take over the reins when his father retired. He was not stupid or incompetent, he simply did not care to be a businessman or devote his life to the job of being next in line for the royal title. He had many interests that he wanted to pursue; being the head of this company felt like a prison to him.

This story does not have a happy ending, and continues as a work in progress. Because the pressure of running the company was so huge, Alan Junior did what he was expected to do. In one heartbreaking talk he said something to the effect of, "I just cannot tell my dad that I want to run a scuba diving business instead of run the family business, he would laugh in my face." He was probably right. Saying no to the throne is not easy; the Prince of Wales did it when he abdicated for the love of Wallis Simpson, but who knows if it was the right thing to do, or just a romantic bewitchment.

Personally I think that if you do not have your heart in your job, you will fail. Maybe it is the state of the economy, but since Alan Junior took over the company it has not done well. Its stocks have fallen dramatically and many wrong-headed decisions have been made, some of such magnitude that they have made the *Wall Street Journal*. An Emperor who does not want his throne is always a disaster.

Allow me one last anecdote. Kyle is also the son of a boss. From his earliest memories he wanted to be the top gun at the firm. Kyle also always draws the Emperor card reversed. Why? Because despite his complete commitment to being the boss, he is just terrible at it. He likes the title, the lifestyle, and his engraved business cards that say PRESIDENT on them. But he is an empty suit. Under all the posturing he is clueless. He has no vision for the company; he just has a vision for himself, and it begins and ends with a corner office and a pretty secretary.

As I hope you see, when deciphering the Emperor card, you step into some difficult waters. You are dealing with big egos, power plays, and father–son expectations. Perhaps the clearest portrayal of the Emperor reversed is exhibited in the movie *Gladiator*. Russell Crowe plays Maximus, a heroic gladiator whose family was murdered at the hands of the corrupt and ineffectual emperor Commodus. Commodus, who has taken the place of his beloved and respected emperor father, is intoxicated with his newfound and seemingly boundless power. Motivated by his bravado and an insane lust to be worshiped by his people, Commodus goes on a reign of terror, ended only when he foolishly challenges Maximus in the gladiator ring and is slain. Commodus is a pitch-perfect example of the Emperor reversed, a seething knot of weak character, misuse of power, and greed.

A final word: Be careful when you read this card. It is not an easy one to offer advice on. You will get in dangerous territory when you identify a deep problem between fathers and sons. Daughters are more likely to verbalize their problems with their mothers. Sons and fathers are another story.

THE HIEROPHANT

THE HIEROPHANT

CARD NUMBER 5

The more that you read, the more things you will know. The more that you learn, the more places you'll go.

—DR. SEUSS

Of all the Major Arcana cards in the tarot deck, the Hierophant can be one of the most confusing to the new client or reader. The concept of the Hierophant is actually quite simple: Literally he symbolizes the pope and is read as a card of organized learning, either at church or synagogue, at school, or through groups dedicated to teaching. But the name *Hierophant* has led to many funny moments for me at the tarot-reading table.

When this card is drawn and placed in a layout, I often get quizzical looks. Once I spent a good half hour with a client trying to explain his profound aptitude for learning, until I noticed him sitting there with a stunned and rather angry look on his face.

I stopped my stream of talking and asked him what was wrong. Encouraging someone to get a master's degree from a good university usually does not bring tears to his eyes.

"I am so offended," he said. "You know I am married, and that I am a family man, and now you want me to believe *I am a hermaphrodite!*" After I calmed him down and assured him that a Hierophant did not mean he had both a penis and a vagina, we continued the reading. I had insulted his manhood, but in the end he was happy to learn that he should continue his higher education.

Another client, a lovely woman with a few extra pounds on her frame, was so self-conscious about her size that she thought the Hierophant was a type of elephant and that I was being mean about her weight problem.

When I read the tarot, it is all too easy for me to get into a groove and extrapolate on the meaning of the cards, ignoring the fact that my client has no idea what I am talking about. I have to take a deep breath and make sure we are both on the same page. In that regard I would make a terrible Hierophant myself, as teaching in a group situation is apparently not my strong suit.

———•———

The term *hierophant* means "one who teaches the holy things"—a religious leader, a shaman, a spiritual guide, a teacher, or a benefactor. This card represents someone of power taking you under her wing and showing you the meaning of life.

This card is to be taken most seriously. Early on during the Fool's journey, he meets the Hierophant as a young impressionable soul. The Fool has already been shaped by the Emperor and Empress, the Magician, and the High Priestess, but the Hierophant is his first formal teacher. The Hierophant captures that moment when we leave the bosom of our family and venture out into the world. Hopefully we will find wise, compassionate teachers who will give us a great foundation for learning. If we fall into the wrong hands, we do not learn but grow increasingly confused and get left behind. In really bad "learning situations," we may become ensnared by cults or groups of deviants with a bad agenda; we will learn through hate and harshness and lose our individuality. Who we learn from is often who we become.

Because the Fool is naive at this point in his journey, he is not a good judge of whom to trust and whom not to. How lucky we are when we align ourselves with great guides or teachers! They can mold our lives, teach us lessons we never forget, and provide a structure that makes us feel safe outside our family. With their help, we learn how to fend for ourselves, and learn what we need to know to get ahead. In the perfect world we would all come out like Eagle Scouts, having mastered all the life skills we need.

If you are represented by the Hierophant dealt right-side up, you have been schooled well. You are on your way to realizing that you are not alone in the universe, and that others share your desire for knowledge and discipline.

Remember when you were around five years old and went to school for the first time? Suddenly there were new authority figures, and you learned that the rules you followed at home were not universal. It was hard to sit still, hard to not go to the bathroom whenever you wanted to. It was hard to understand why picking your nose was not okay, why you had to share a cookie with someone you didn't know, and why you had to raise your hand if you wanted to speak. For some of us this transition came easily; for others it was the first step in a long path of battling rules and regulations, of seeking nonconformity. The Hierophant is not about creativity and individualism, but about formal structure and conforming. Hierophant expressions include "being part of a team" or "being disciplined."

There are some cards that are of immediate significance, and some that have a broader scope. The Hierophant is not for me an immediate card; it will never mean you will suddenly wake up one day and magically have a scope of knowledge, or that you will instantaneously know the profound and arcane mysteries of a belief system. The Hierophant card works slowly. It is not like getting a spray tan . . . you can't walk into the booth white and come out bronze. Instead the Hierophant card is hard, sometimes tedious, work, but the payoff is that you become a card-carrying member of a greater society and the master of a task.

The Hierophant card is about starting in the mailroom of life and working your way up, about being a plebe, a probie, a freshman, or simply wet behind the ears. The pope is a metaphor in this card in that being God's go-to guy on earth is a long but rewarding process. You can't just buy the cool hat and proclaim yourself pope. Well, I guess you could, but you might be carted off to the funny farm.

Like all the Major Arcana cards, the Hierophant has multiple meanings, yet they all stay within the same parameters. It might be more accurate to say that in addition to getting an education and being part of a church, the Hierophant is very much about whom you choose to ally yourself with. This card is often a marker of a good marriage union, and about placing yourself squarely in with the right crowd.

My mother often said to me, "If you lie down with dogs, you get up with fleas," meaning that if I continued to hang around with the bad crowd or the outcasts I adored, I too would bear that label. Of course I thought my mother was an idiot. At fifteen, is there any other way to see your mother? It took me many years and much maturity to understand what she meant.

In the fullness of time, the people my mother did not like turned out to be (to cut to the chase) losers. They were shiftless liars, petty shoplifters, and dope "fiends." I thought they were wildly glamorous, while she just saw them as a dead end. My mother knew how easy it was to get me off track at fifteen years old and how impressionable I was, and she knew that with a few exceptions people who exhibit bad behavior keep doing so all their lives.

I grew up many decades ago when life was much milder, even in Midtown Manhattan where I was raised. Stealing a lipstick from the drugstore or smoking a cigarette was a major crime to my parents and their cronies, and if I or my friends were caught we faced a hanging judge and no plea bargaining. Needless to say the opportunities to go off the right track in life are much more varied these days.

Sometimes the card has a deeper meaning. It can warn the reader to watch out for clients who are in some sort of unhealthy captivity. I do not mean they are nailed in a box, but that they have somehow drifted off into a relationship or a job that makes them feel utterly stuck.

A friend of mine has been waging an internal war to find the gumption to break up with her philandering married boy-friend. In her own words, she is "waiting for him to give her permission to go." Huh? I couldn't believe what I was hearing. She has chosen to abdicate choice in the matter, instead waiting for him to say he does not need her around anymore. I suspect this "freedom" will be a long time coming, if ever. Why let a slave out of her shackles if you still might need her down the road?

The Hierophant can also point to a client being a spiritual miser. This doesn't refer to donating to charities or paying tithes; the Hierophant rather reminds us to give of ourselves as a shoulder to lean on or a hand to hold. Many people find it easier to scribble out a check than find the time to patiently listen to a friend's plight. With the Hierophant card we must time and again remind ourselves that we lead by example; the grace we give to others comes back manyfold to us. We take wisdom from our teachers, but it is our job to teach what we know to others. The cycle should never end, but flow like a stream.

THE LOVERS

THE LOVERS

CARD NUMBER 6

The hunger for love is much more difficult to remove than the hunger for bread.

—MOTHER TERESA

The Lovers card is straightforward yet provocative. It is the card that a reader hopes to get when asked for the nine-million-five-hundred-thousandth time that month by a client if she will soon find love. How can it possibly be that so many people are looking for love? Time and again I sit across from female clients—who by any logical measure are young, smart, beautiful, wealthy, and charming—who tell me they can't find a decent man. Notice I have not said that male clients have this question. For the guys, if they question their love life at all, it involves whether the wife will find out about the mistress.

Not so long ago I did a reading for a group of four girl-friends. They looked like Charlie's Angels, or the *Sex and the*

City gang, all gorgeous, clever, funny, and accomplished: a redhead, two blondes, and a raven-haired stunner. Every single one of them had the same question; the only question she truly cared about . . . when was Mr. Right going to come her way? And voilà, they all drew the Lovers card reversed, which means he had yet to appear on the radar. For someone already seeing a man, the card means he is bad news and nothing will come of the relationship.

I have lived long enough to remember when men did the hunting, when even wallflowers and Miss Lonely-Hearts wound up with someone to keep her feet warm in bed (and I do not mean a cat). As car dealers put it, "There is an ass for every seat." Everyone found someone, they got married, and they stayed married. Now I hear the following lament over and over: "I am seeing a married man, he says he is getting a divorce but it has been seven years already, should I trust him?" Or, "My husband and I never have sex anymore, he looks at porn on the computer all night and I have a crush on the UPS man." Or, "I love my husband, but I do not *love* him . . . if you know what I mean."

Yes, I know what you mean, but do you?

———•———

The first bit of advice I have to offer is that love is not easy (even sex is not easy, but I will get to that in a minute). The male and female on the Lovers card look painfully out of step in this modern world. Eve does not have double-D boob implants; Adam is not pierced and his hair is not shaved or spiky with "product." Here is what you must know, the secret to love that I have learned over the years.

1. IT IS NOT YOUR FAULT THAT YOU CANNOT FIND A MAN!
2. IT IS TOTALLY YOUR FAULT THAT YOU CANNOT FIND A MAN!

Is this confusing? You bet, but so is life in the twenty-first century. Let me take both statements and explain what I mean.

Statement 1: Blame it on reality TV shows, *Playboy, Hustler,* "sexting," strip clubs, Facebook, YouTube, and the Internet. As a unit they have skewed men's view of what they *think* they deserve. Even the most repulsive men find themselves judging perfectly acceptable females as inadequate. To these self-styled princes in their imaginary harems, most real women are too flat-chested (breast implants please), too fat (these days a size 10 is plus-size), too hairy (one Brazilian wax coming up), too demanding (what do you mean, get married?), too boring (where's Paris Hilton?), and too old (I can't date anyone over twenty-four). Who makes these lists? No, not international playboys or billionaires, we are talking about the guy who works all day behind the counter at the 7-Eleven (if he works at all), wears stained T-shirts with silly mottos, has a beer gut, and thinks nothing of belching or farting as nature calls. Mr. Slobbo now thinks that he pretty much deserves Pamela Anderson or Tila Tequila as his Saturday-night date.

The really pathetic part of all this is that should Pam or Tila magically turn up at his door, he would not have a clue what to do with her, other than have sex. This modern man has not only lost the simple art of courtship but has come to devalue women in general.

And why should he do anything when women are so desperate to get his attention? Let the girls fight it out among themselves, and if he is really lucky there will be a good cat-fight in public with lots of name calling and hair pulling. Wow, will his reputation as a stud rise among his friends!

Now, let me move on to the second statement, the one where you *are* to blame. As a tarot reader I now hear stories that ten or twenty years ago might have made me wonder about my client's mental capacity or consider if she had been brainwashed by a cult. Could these beautiful, wealthy, and accomplished women across the table from me, weeping copiously into my Kleenex, really have no clue that (romantically) actions speak louder than words? When I hear a sentence start with "Yes, but he said . . . ," I try to take a deep breath and remain calm because I know that it is now time for the Big Denial Show to begin. The overture is playing and the curtain begins to rise.

An attractive woman walks center stage. She is trying to look jaunty and in control, and then she begins reading her lines. She is a really good actress, could teach Meryl Streep a thing or two. She truly wants to believe and have me believe the following about the man she is crazily in love with . . .

Yes, but he doesn't sleep with his wife anymore.

Yes, but he is in the process of divorce.

Yes, but he only sees other women for sex, he loves *me*.

Yes, but although I have been with him for twenty years he says he isn't ready for marriage.

Yes, but he *is* looking for work. I am just helping him out financially.

Yes, but he really loves me, he just needs a green card to stay in the country.

Yes, but it was just a loan, and no I didn't have him sign anything.

Yes, but I have never been to his house because he says it is being painted (for five years).

Yes, but he says he adores my four kids from my previous marriages.

Yes, he has a bad temper, but a lot of it is my fault.

If you see yourself in this woman, I applaud you. Not for your insight but for your acting ability. It is hard work to pretend that all is fine when it so clearly isn't.

People who come to me to read their cards often mistake me for a magician. They think or hope that I can cast a spell and make recalcitrant men fall madly in love with them, make ex-wives vanish into the ether, and produce engagement rings from thin air. I can't do this. What I can do is hold up a mirror and show them how they look to the outside world, that they are worthy of love but also in denial. I call a spade a spade. If they are deluding themselves, I gently tell them so. Do my clients hear me? Yes, but it takes time to sink in. Often they walk away annoyed or tell me I do not understand the situation. Then six months or a year down the road comes the contrite phone call confirming what I said as true.

In many decks of tarot cards, specifically the Tarot of Prague deck that I so often use, the Lovers are under the protective wings of a benevolent angel who hovers over them. She unfurls a banner that says NOTHING BETTER HERE BELOW—that is, despite having been kicked out of the Garden of Eden, life is still wonderful when you are in love. What does this symbolism mean? Is love holy, blessed, and a gift from God? There are many interpretations of this image, but my personal one is that no matter how hard you may try— with all the caveats and "yes buts" to pretend love is love when it is not—the big angel is a sign that we have no real power or influence over love. It is a gift from something higher than us; one given without ulterior motives, schemes, or deviousness. To be in love is a link to something greater; it is a glimpse of being blessed and holy. It is not based on anything but what it is . . . love. And if you think you control that vehicle, pull over because you are on a road to nowhere.

If you want to challenge this card's veracity, substitute another figure for the towering angel. How about a gigantic matrimonial lawyer holding a pre-nup? Or maybe a controlling mother who will only be happy if you marry for wealth or status? Imagine a huge demanding teenager looming over the couple, or your high school soccer coach who told you that you were not good enough to make the team. It is a ridiculous notion, but oddly many of us allow extraneous others to dictate our romantic lives. The tarot deck is not so blockheaded that it does not take into account how other aspects of our existence color it, but *color* is different from *control*. For this reason I never do single card readings. Reading a single card is like serving someone a sprig of tarragon with their steak rather than a béarnaise sauce. A single card is but one ingredient in the complicated recipe of our lives.

When the Lovers card comes up in a spread—let's say it is even the central card—the reader must look at what cards are around it. Usually there are moderating issues such as angry parents, money problems, lack of commitment, sexual problems, having children or not, moving far away—that sort of thing. I have had clients ask me what color dresses their bridesmaids should wear, or if they should go with a traditional cake versus cupcakes. I can assure you that the deck has no clue about these questions. The arcane nature of the deck does not include pastry or the color blue. The tarot is a big-issue adviser; if you need help with the wedding flowers, get a copy of *Brides* magazine, don't call me.

The Lovers card isn't only about the highest spiritual kind of love. It is a down-and-dirty card about passionate sex. There are times (after a long day of sitting across the table from people) when I truly believe that absolutely no one in America has sex anymore. Let me amend this: Lots of people are having sex or wanting to have sex, just not with their spouse. However, since only I have this devastating overview, I can't just plunk it on the table and expect my client to believe it. We have to get into it sideways, with the client foofing and fussing about what a wonderful provider and best friend her husband is, but then in sotto voce sharing, "We never have sex anymore." At this point I am supposed to show great shock, but as I already know what is coming I am mentally filing my nails.

The truth is that for many people, sexual heat only lasts a few years in a marriage. The lucky few for whom the eternal flame never dies are in the happy minority. I know a few long-married couples well into their senior years who are such bed breakers that it is almost funny. It has nothing at all to do with either spouse being attractive. Some of my celibate clients are movie-star beautiful, bodies toned to perfection, hair streaked with gold, dressed by the best designers, but to their husbands they are far less attractive than the high-definition fifty-two-inch TV in the den with the football game on. And don't think women are the only ones let down romantically and sexually in marriage. Often Mr. Invisible comes home after an ass-busting day at the office to find his wife still at work herself or out playing golf, the kids grunting hello at him with a request for money as they rush out the door to see their friends. I asked a client once what her husband did for work. She smiled brightly and said, "I'm really not sure, he has an office somewhere."

These are the people who are at high risk for having affairs, and over my long career as a tarot card reader I could count on half a hand the affairs predicated on this desperation that led to marriage and a happier life. In other words, affairs do not work; the majority of affairs are dead ends, a Band-Aid for a weeping wound that is not easily healed.

As I've mentioned, I sometimes use the cards like a Rorschach test: I flip the tables on my clients and have them look at their cards and tell me what they see. I don't tell them what reversals mean, or which cards are ominous or bright. The results are sometimes startling. No matter what deck of cards I use, I'm always astounded at the strong reaction to the Lovers card. "They look miserable," "They look embarrassed," "He's not looking at her," "The cloud between them signifies danger," "Who's that big person glaring down at them?" "The hot sun must mean they are in the Caribbean on their honeymoon," "Why is the snake behind her and not him?" "The peaked mountain behind them symbolizes his erection" . . . and so on. Is it any wonder the psychoanalyst Carl Jung was crazy for the tarot deck? It truly is the golden road into the unconscious.

The way to utilize the Lovers card in a reading is to let it lead you. Let it slowly pull your true feelings about your partner out. Let the reader say your words back to you. Sit quietly and listen, let your defenses go. The cards are Rosetta stones, and you are the only one who can decipher them. You can never fool the deck. You may be able to fool your friends and yourself, and in some instances even the reader, but not the deck. If you don't want a straight answer from the deck, don't ask.

Can you make someone love you? No. Can you make yourself love someone else? Not much. Can you live without either being loved or loving a partner? It is probably the hardest task on this earth, but you can, and in the long run clearing your closets of relationships that no longer work is frightening but an utter necessity. The worst thing that can happen is you are the only one left in the equation, and you must learn to love yourself. Most of us have no clue what this means or how to do it. When one relationship ends, we act like passengers on the *Titanic* rushing into the few available lifeboats. To not feel like losers, we haunt the matchmaking websites, we go to bars or singles events dressed to the nines, predatory and on the make. Our desperation surrounds us like heavy perfume. Our eyes dart around crazily looking for Mr. Right, or Mr. Right Now. *Pick me, pick me,* we plead internally when we see someone who vaguely might fit the bill.

When we start this mating behavior coming out of a shattered relationship, we have high standards: We want a rich man, or a compassionate doctor, or George Clooney's twin brother, or someone with a charge account at Cartier. After a few months on the hunt, we're ready to settle for anyone with four limbs and no serious criminal record. We text him, snoop on him, dig for clues about his feelings, plot revenge on his other female acquaintances, consider using voodoo, and get liposuction. And the more we do this, the less attractive we become to the object of our desire. Somehow men (or women) who are the target of such fatal attraction sense it, know it, and will run screaming from it. That is, if they're lucky. If you are mesmerized and "in love" with a sociopath, being lonely is the least of your problems; you may also wind up penniless and emotionally broken.

One of the most powerful layouts is a Lovers card next to or above the Fool card. This is a not a sign that you have been a fool in love, but rather that it's time to tear down the house of your old behaviors and rebuild it brick by brick. Again, the first person you must learn to love is yourself. This is hard work. When I do phone readings and a client describes herself as looking somewhere between Quasimodo and the Elephant Man, and then we meet in person and she is a 12 on the 1-to-10 gorgeous scale, I shake my head in despair. Few women like themselves, much less love themselves. We like parts of ourselves: our eyelashes, our feet, or maybe we have a decent tennis serve. We think we are not good enough— too fat, too stupid, too old—and the only way no one will notice what complete losers we are is if we have a man on our arm to disguise and deflect our basic hideousness. This is wrong.

One last word of advice: I like to dissuade my clients from the hackneyed old phrase, "All the good ones are taken." Not only is this not true, but it is a very juvenile way of looking at the world and will get you nowhere. Yes, we all see and admire long-term partners, couples who despite the odds and the struggles have stayed together not out of duty but out of desire. But don't for a minute think this is commonplace. I remember as an obnoxious young teenager whining every complaint to my mother this way: "But *everyone* has . . ." The list was long and in retrospect horrid, a litany of lime-green Pappagallo shoes, mohair sweaters, a certain hideous chintz skirt with cabbage roses on it that all the girls in the clique wore one spring, and a necklace with a heart-shaped pendant that you wore half of and gave your best friend the other half. My mother (having no doubt read the same script as every other mother in America) countered with "If all the popular girls jumped off the Brooklyn Bridge, would you?" Yes, I probably would have if it ensured popularity and a date with a cute guy.

The point of this bit of nostalgia is that *everyone* does not have a wonderful boyfriend or a devoted husband, *everyone* is not sexually satisfied, *everyone* does not get roses and diamonds on Valentine's Day. This is teenage thinking at its most destructive, and if you let your mind go down this path you will make yourself more miserable than you ever imagined.

So how do you find love? You don't, it finds you. The trick is to allow yourself to know it when you see it. The metaphorical puffy chintz skirt with the cabbage roses may not appeal to you now, and maybe the man of your dreams needs an update as well. Love might not look like you pictured it, but that too is a sign of maturity. Finding love is the easiest task in the world because it means you can stop trying so hard. Believe that the universe cherishes you (even if you don't). Stop thinking only of yourself and be kind to others. Wonder at the perfection of nature, laugh at your foibles, and make yourself useful. Be happy that you once had love even if you don't have it now. Feed your soul and your spirit and love will find you. Of this I am sure.

THE CHARIOT

THE CHARIOT

CARD NUMBER 7

But at my back I always hear
Time's winged chariot hurrying near;
And yonder all before us lie
Deserts of vast eternity.

—ANDREW MARVELL

Modern life doesn't look much like life did five hundred years ago when the tarot became popular, but this card's reckless young man behind a horse, a sphinx, or the wheel of a hot car hasn't changed much over the centuries. The Chariot card lands smack in the middle between the Lovers and Strength. It is a young person's card, showing the Fool at a still-early point in his journey, riddled with testosterone and flushed with youthful energy. Having just left the Lovers card where he was introduced to the intoxicating joy of sexual passion, he now gets behind the wheel to make tracks fast.

In many decks the Chariot card shows the struggle to keep the team of animals or entities together in a straight line. Anyone who has ever driven a team of horses knows this is a learned and difficult skill. Why should two or four or six animals want to go in the same direction? It is against nature, and depends on the ability of the driver to gain control. The Budweiser Clydesdales make it look easy, but if you try to direct 20,000 pounds of recalcitrant horses you will understand the art of driving a team.

And so it is with life. Have you ever been with a husband, wife, best friend, mother, or father who wants to do the same thing as you all the time? At best we compromise and give and take a little to meet on an acceptable common ground. I have eavesdropped many times on conversations that go like this:

GIRLFRIEND #1: Have you seen the new movie with Cameron Diaz?

GIRLFRIEND #2: I don't like her, she has shifty eyes.

GIRLFRIEND #3: I want to see the new James Bond movie.

GIRLFRIEND #1: I hate anything with guns.

GIRLFRIEND #2: What about the one with that cute guy from the last movie we saw, what's his name?

GIRLFRIEND #3: I saw it already.

WAITER: Ladies, here is your check.

GIRLFRIEND #1: I'll put it on my credit card, you can give me cash.

GIRLFRIEND #2: I don't have cash, can I write you a check?

GIRLFRIEND #3: You owe me money from the last meal when I paid.

GIRLFRIEND #2: I don't remember that!

And on and on it goes, indicating that getting even a small group of people to agree on anything is like herding cats.

The Chariot is not a card I especially like to work with because its meanings can be so slippery, even more so if dealt reversed. It is also a card relating to my least favorite of the ten deadly sins: pride.

Personally I can't stand braggarts and pompous sorts. Boasting is lost on me, and snobbery feels poisonous. Truthfully, don't we just love to see guys like that fall on their faces?

The saving grace of the Chariot is that the Fool is still a youth, and we give more leeway to the young and brash than the mature and obnoxious. In mythology Apollo the sun god rode in his chariot across the sky each day, creating daytime from dawn to dusk. His son Phaeton pleaded with Dad for the keys to the chariot and finally, after the kind of nagging only teenagers can do, Apollo agreed to let him go for a ride. Phaeton drove the chariot recklessly all over the sky, scorching parts of the earth when he came too close, letting others freeze as he veered away from them. Finally Zeus had had enough of seeing this young man wreak havoc on his earthly realm and sent a thunderbolt right at Phaeton, who fell to earth dead. Obviously there was no driver's ed in Greek mythology.

The Chariot card can be a formidable indicator of daredevils, reckless people, and those whose egos are out of control. The Chariot can also indicate a warrior, not a brave defender of his land but a hothead who is always ready to rumble. This card depicts the kind of folks you pray will never cross your path, because if they do they will hit you, sue you, or run you over on the way to where they want to go. If 500-year-old cards can signify road rage, this one does.

Although there are many positive interpretations of the Chariot, when I read they usually do not apply. Maybe it's me, maybe my clients, but it is rarely a good card. The Chariot right-side up can be a sign of providence, of being well taken care of. You will have what you need, the crops will grow, your product will find a market and your dreams a home. But in my readings the Chariot likes to stand on its head, indicating that a client has problems with anger, is looking for trouble, and is longing to go to war. If the Chariot right-side up indicates Mel Gibson's heroic character in the movie *Braveheart,* flipped upside down it can be the real Mel Gibson, ranting and raving and being an out-of-control bastard.

I have drawn the Chariot reversed with a few lawyers I read for. Although there are other law-related cards in the deck, this one is very active for this particular subset of clients, and it makes me slightly nauseous. I hate how our litigious society awards money to people who sue because their coffee was too hot or no one told them they should not eat shampoo. This sort of legal back-and-forth can very much relate to the Chariot—in short, a big ado about nothing.

The Chariot right-side up can also be about vengeance, especially as it pertains to vehicles. How does this translate into modern society? I would say slashing a tire, keying a car, or giving the finger to someone who cuts you off on the highway all apply. The Chariot is often a card not of major conflicts, but of the minor ones that make us miserable.

You may be wondering if I am leaving out the obvious interpretation of a gladiator driving a golden carriage through the streets, triumphant. Yes, this card can mean victory, but you should also know that it demands hubris. In ancient Rome when a gladiator rode through the city after winning a battle, a slave rode on the back of his carriage to hold the laurel wreath over his head. The slave was also there to keep up a running dialogue, reminding the hero that the gods were watching him; if he acted as their equal, they would destroy him. Wouldn't it be great if all hedge fund managers were followed everywhere by some lackey whose job it was to tell them to get over themselves!

When we grow older patience, holding our tongue, and well-thought-out actions come naturally. Asking a teenager to do this is like asking a cow to ice-skate. Maybe it is the raging hormones or the still-undeveloped part of the brain that makes taking things slowly so difficult, but if you are dealing with young people you must take them as they are in this stage of development. They do not understand how to naturally control impulsivity, and they must learn it slowly. If you are a grown-up stuck in this stage, you need to change.

One final interpretation of this card is based on the connection between the charioteer and the animals that pull him along. My favorite tarot image is the two sphinxes that pull the chariot. Do you (like me) just adore the concept of a sphinx? Even the word *sphinx* is magical; there is no other word quite like it. (I refute one tarot historian's contention that the word *sphincter* comes from this word. My claim is based on absolutely nothing more than not wanting my favorite woman/beast to have any relation to one's smelly guts.)

The important thing to know about a sphinx is that she is half human and half animal. The Chariot card is about controlling our impulsive sides, and this can be a lesson in not allowing ourselves to act with the unbridled passion of the animals that we evolutionarily descended from. Animals are ruled by survival: They must kill or be killed, they must eat and procreate. Animals are not contemplative, but operate on a linear progression from one day to the next. This is why animals often do not do well in captivity. Providing all their needs takes away the whole point of their lives. No animal ever thinks, *Thank God my meals are taken care of, so now I have time to work on my hobbies.* When animals have "downtime," they often wither and die.

The sphinx, in addition to being half human, half beast, is the keeper of secrets. I can think of nothing that the tarot deck likes more than a good secret. The very phrase *Major Arcana* means "big secrets." Historically people who held the big secrets ruled the world. I always think that one of the reasons conspiracy theories continue to blossom is that by nature people like to think someone out there holds the keys to the secret kingdom, sharing it with the anointed few.

In mythology travelers had to answer the riddle of the sphinx to get where they were going. It was very likely that impetuous travelers were not let through because they were too antsy to give it real thought. The sphinx gave her blessing only to those whose minds were in gear. This is a hard lesson for the still-young Fool to learn. He wants to go zero to sixty, but life demands that he slow down and enjoy the scenery lest he arrive at his final destination with no lessons learned. His tires will be as bald as his old man's head, and the trip over before it began.

STRENGTH

STRENGTH

CARD NUMBER 8

Confront the dark parts of yourself, and work to banish them with illumination and forgiveness. Your willingness to wrestle with your demons will cause your angels to sing. Use the pain as fuel, as a reminder of your strength.

—AUGUST WILSON

If I were directing a movie instead of writing this book, I'd contrast the Chariot and the Strength cards like this:

The Scene: A dark alley somewhere in the city at night. A gang of tough kids is hanging out, looking for trouble.

PUNK #1: Hey! Here comes a guy who just wants to give us his wallet!

A sad-looking victim is set upon by the gang, roughed up, and robbed.

PUNK #2: Look at Grandma and Grandpa shuffling this way, let's get them!

An elderly couple walks slowly toward the gang. They too are mugged and sent on their way without their watch and wallet.

PUNK #3: Look at this loser, let's get him.

An unassuming man walks toward the gang whistling a tune softly, hands in his pockets.

PUNK #1: Hey jerk-off, give us your money!

The unassuming man takes off his jacket and with karate kicks, kung fu, superhero jumps, blazing fists, and rib-cracking flying attacks beats the bloody tar out of the punks, leaving them groaning on the ground and begging for help.

Okay, so I will never make it as a Hollywood director, and of course I shamelessly lifted this scene from about 10,000 movies I have seen where Bruce Lee, Chuck Norris, Charles Bronson, Jackie Chan, or Mr. Miyagi does what we all wish we could do.

The Strength card represents the unassuming hero who does not flaunt his powers but can call on them when the need is there. The Chariot (in its worst incarnation) is the bullies.

With this card, *strength* does not refer to pumping iron at the gym or a contest to see who can pull a cement truck with his teeth. In older decks of tarot cards, this card was called Fortitude, representing someone who could draw on mental resources to get through tough times.

Whether right-side up or reversed, the Strength card is not subtle. Right-side up it is a wonderful reflection of someone who is courageous, powerful in the best sense of the word, and generous in helping others. Reversed it can mirror the lesser aspects of the Chariot, pointing to someone who is weak or abusive in her role as leader.

An image of a lion is often shown for this card, reflecting the metaphor of being "lionhearted," or brave in all things. It would be easy to think this card is only drawn by soldiers, policemen, or firefighters who on a daily basis risk their lives. Yet in my experience this card is often drawn by the meekest of my clients, people who are acting heroically with their personal challenges.

Say hello to Savannah. When I first met Savannah, she had not left her house in ten years. This severely troubled agoraphobic would have a level 10 panic attack even contemplating going outside her home. Like most phobic people Savannah was very bright; her fears had nothing to do with her intelligence. As a therapist who worked with phobic people once told me, you have to be very creative to think of all the reasons why you cannot do something.

Because she lived in another state, I did phone readings with Savannah. Although she was wonderful to work with, we were not making much progress in getting her on the other side of her front door. The Strength card always made an appearance in her readings, and when I told her I was looking at it she would snort and say defensively, "If I am so strong, why can't I walk to my mailbox without feeling like I am going to die?"

Fortunately, she was working with a very good therapist and was on medication, enough to take the edge off the raw terror and make the needed steps to recovery without being swayed by the drama of her condition. After a year she was driving around the city in which she lived, and had twice gone to the movies. This was huge. Of course her shrink (and I) wanted to claim her success as coming from our wise counsel. I asked her on the phone what was the final thing that gave her the courage to leave the house.

"My sneakers," she said.

"Excuse me?" I said, thinking I had misunderstood her.

"My sneakers," she repeated. "I was wearing a pair of Nike sneakers, and when I was about to put one foot out the door I looked at that boomerang-like logo and remembered their ad, 'Just Do It!' So I did." Some people attempt bravery by being in a foxhole on the front line of a war, some people by placing one sneakered foot in front of another. In my opinion they are both heroic.

The Strength card often comes up for people battling addictions or illness. It is a sign that they do have the fortitude to conquer their difficulties. When someone starts out with a huge emotional or physical adversary, she feels like Daniel in the lion's den: tiny, outmatched, and underequipped for battle. The metaphorical lion (cigarettes, cancer, alcohol, what have you) is circling with the clear message that it will kill you. If fear is all you can come up with as an armament, you are going to make some lion a very quick and tasty lunch. If you can feel the fear, let it wash over you, and then do what you have to do to defend yourself, you have a fighting chance of survival.

Now for a word or two on disrespecting fear and its consequences. Remember the mauling that Roy of the act Siegfried and Roy took on the Las Vegas stage from one of his white tigers? Newspaper headlines screamed "freak accident," and people wrung their hands, asking how it could have happened. I think Roy lost his fear.

People who work with animals fall under the delusion that they are in complete control. They are either masters with a top hat and a whip, or they feel that they and the animals have an understanding, that they are friends and should be treated accordingly. Aside from Roy, I think of crocodile expert Steve Irwin stung to death while swimming with a stingray; Timothy Treadwell, the subject of the documentary film *Grizzly Man,* who was eaten by one of his "friendly" bears; and the woman who was ripped to shreds by Travis, her neighbor's pet chimpanzee. Now, please do not misunderstand me; I love animals beyond reason. But I also know that they are not humans and at any time can act like, well, animals. I have been on the back of a perfectly mannered horse that decided for no apparent reason to dump me on my face on an asphalt road. I have seen tamed circus elephants stampede and cuddly dogs bite people. The point of all this is that there is a big difference between being brave and strong and being delusional. The task is to find a comfortable place between being scared of everything and frightened of nothing.

———•———

One other important aspect of the Strength card is compassion. This card usually shows a gentle woman holding the lion's mouth, not a bold man. I honestly don't know if people are born with compassion or if it is a learned behavior, but it is what separates man and beast. I don't think the tiger that attempted to eat Roy thought, *Ah shucks, maybe the poor guy is having a hard day; I'll give him a pass.* I don't think the tiger thought of anything except that killing Roy seemed like the thing to do at that moment. If clients draw the Strength card, I investigate whether they need to help someone. Helping people is a funny thing; many people either rush headlong into it or withdraw from it, thinking that it will consume them.

I remember many years back working with a young woman who was startlingly compassionless. Naomi was the daughter of a psychologist and a social worker, and I assumed her emotional bluntness might have been a result of hearing one too many stories of needy people around the dinner table.

This is the way Naomi presented herself to me:

JANE: How's college?

NAOMI: Fine.

JANE: Have you made friends?

NAOMI: I don't have time for friends, they suck you dry.

JANE: I don't understand?

NAOMI: (*puts on a whiny voice*) Oh Naomi can you lend me your lecture notes, Oh Naomi can you drive me into town, Oh Naomi can I borrow your blue sweater.

JANE: You find that annoying?

NAOMI: Unbearable.

Later that year Naomi's father was shot to death in his office in an attempted robbery. She returned to school in a funk and was amazed at the kind words spoken to her by her classmates. Arms of people she had ignored hugged her, people shed tears with her, and her roommate made a little shrine in their shared room with a candle before Naomi's father's picture. Through the most unfortunate of events, Naomi learned the blessing of compassion. She knew she had not "earned it" from her classmates, but they still chose to be there for her. In her time of need, she borrowed strength from other people.

The Strength card reversed is an all-too-familiar person: the petty tyrant. This includes the teacher who bullies her students, the boss from hell, even a spouse who wields too much negative power. People like this leave a mark on us way out of proportion to their true role in our lives. The more sensitive you are, the more easily you can be bruised by this sort of person. I remember from my own youth a gym teacher who made a spectacle out of my inability to vault over the leather "horse." These small acts of meanness stick with us. If you are in a position to make someone of lesser rank than you miserable, think twice before you indulge yourself. It may seem like an exercise of strength, but it is an abuse of power that will come back to bite you over the years.

The best show of strength is to intervene when you see another person needlessly humiliated. I am not talking about stopping a bar fight or risking danger, but if you are seeing someone being berated and embarrassed, do not be afraid to speak up. You will like yourself afterward.

Toxic people sap our strength. Like Samson, who lost his power when Delilah cut off his hair, letting people walk roughshod over us or others leaves us feeling sapped. Negative energy is like poison.

THE HERMIT

THE HERMIT

CARD NUMBER 9

We're born alone, we live alone, and we die alone. Only through our love and friendship can we create the illusion for the moment that we're not alone.

—ORSON WELLES

When I lecture on tarot and I come to the Hermit card, I show two slides: one of the French existentialist philosopher Jean-Paul Sartre, the other of Nelson Mandela. The Hermit card represents solitude and introspective thought. Classically, this card demands that the person who draws it needs to retreat from society and think things over, and then come back to the fold and tell the world what he has learned.

Many people like being alone. Alone is different than lonely, which pretty much nobody likes. Alone gives us downtime to think our thoughts and commune with our inner selves. It allows our minds to wander, to solve questions, and to touch the creative center of our soul. Introverts know this.

I often wonder if the next generation will ever have the opportunity for quiet. What we do nowadays when we are alone is socialize like mad via Internet or cell phone. As the world gets noisier and more complicated, most of us just want some downtime to relax, but the more philosophical types will also use solitude as a way to look within.

The Fool (who never misses a chance to learn something from his journey) has at this point become a philosophical fellow. Until meeting up with the Hermit, the Fool has been bedazzled by everything bright and shiny around him—but now he finds it imperative to look inward. Children and adolescents do not naturally soul-search; this behavior is learned later in life and is a major part of maturity. At this stage in our journey through life, we are no longer content to simply see what our peers are doing and emulate them. We instead step back and confront (perhaps for the very first time) what is right for us, what our inner voice says. Seems easy? It is not.

Introspection is not a natural human condition. I recently reread Tobias Schneebaum's startling 1955 travel memoir *Keep the River to Your Right,* describing his forays deep into the Peruvian forest where he became part of a tribe of cannibalistic headhunters. This is not fiction but a man's true life story. Schneebaum lived among the tribal natives, doing as they did (including eating the heart of an enemy), and it was on this trip that he found his true inner being. What struck me even more than how a nice Jewish boy from New York became a cannibal manqué was his discovery that empathy and soul searching were virtually nonexistent among these Stone Age–style people. Happiness, sexuality, anger, and grief were all there and fully operative, but soul searching was not. Because most of us do not operate on Stone Age values, but rather as sophisticated modern sorts, we are beset with dozens of different versions of the "what if," "should I," and "what does it all mean" thoughts.

Looking inward is what separates modern man from primitive man. Probably the truest exposition of this painful journey is existential philosopher Jean-Paul Sartre's 1938 novel *Nausea*. If Sartre had never written the book but only come up with the title, I think he would still deserve the Nobel Prize that he famously declined. Looking inward is often violently unpleasant, disturbing, and positively vomit making. In *Nausea* the protagonist Antoine Roquentin retires to a seaside village in France to conclude his scholarly work. Slowly but surely the world at large begins to disgust him. He disgusts himself; every sight and smell and object in his diminishing world becomes repulsive to him. At first he feels the need to talk to others about this queasy feeling, but then he withdraws and decides to keep it within. Of course, it grows worse.

Nausea may be the official handbook for Hermits, with lines like "I live alone, entirely alone. I never speak to anyone, never; I receive nothing, I give nothing"; and "I tear myself from the window and stumble across the room; I glue myself against the looking glass. I stare at myself, I disgust myself; one more eternity. Finally I flee from my image. I watch the ceiling, I'd like to sleep."

Turning now away from a self-styled cannibal and the world's most depressing philosopher, let me say a word about Nelson Mandela. As a resistance fighter against apartheid in South Africa, Mandela spent a total of twenty-seven years in prison, where he spent every day thinking, planning, and learning how to further his cause. As a political prisoner he was at the bottom of the prison system, granted only one visitor and one letter every six months. His time was spent breaking rocks in a lime quarry, but still he managed by correspondence course to earn a bachelor of laws degree from the University of London. Alone most of the time in a bleak little cell, he was warmed by the infrequent visits by the Red Cross, whom he saw as "a beacon of humanity within the dark inhumane world of political imprisonment." Even for those who do not share his political beliefs, Mandela is the uncontested symbol of a man who utterly alone and stripped of his external humanity used every precious moment wisely, and flourished.

———•———

It is impossible to look inward and be introspective at the same time you are in a rowdy group or overwhelmed with what you are watching at the movies or on TV. The Hermit card can be misread as a card that shows the client winding up a lonely spinster or an old bachelor living in a rooming house. I see clients flinch when it hits the table. The severe image of the Hermit shown at the start of this chapter from the Bohemian Gothic Tarot deck is not what we would care to look like. It is thus important to bring these ancient cards into a modern context. Two hundred years ago it was popular for very wealthy aristocrats in the English countryside to allow a hermit to take up residence on their land. Often these hermits lived in a cave or a small lean-to on the property, and they kept to themselves. The hermit was a sort of living lawn ornament, a pastoral decoration like a gazing ball or a pink flamingo. To contemplate his simple lonely existence made the lords and ladies who lived in the giant estates feel somehow more connected to the simple things in life. Having a property so vast that a hermit could take up residence on it and not be bothered was a strange but true status symbol.

Most of us do not have a resident hermit on our property, do we? I think back to a lovely client of mine named Theodora, who lived on a big hunk of property with a gorgeous house plunked in the middle of it. Her husband was a neurosurgeon, made a ton of money, and was looked up to by everyone in the community. Both Theodora and her husband were blond and tall and looked like they'd stepped out of a Ralph Lauren advertisement.

My first session with Theodora was one of those slippery deals that I find very frustrating. I honestly did not know why she wanted a reading. Everything was fine, more than fine, and maybe a little too perfect. She loved her husband, swore he loved her and their three kids, and told me repeatedly that as soon as he was through with work he rushed home.

Having sat across the table from endless sagas of husbands who, when they are through with work, go directly to a pub, a club, or a golf course, I could not see what Theodora was getting at. As it turned out, her husband did indeed come flying home from work every day, not even stopping to put gas in the car. But this was the scenario: He threw his coat on a chair, went into their bedroom, changed into sweatpants and a T-shirt, and descended to their finished basement, where he played war games on the computer until 5:00 a.m. the following day. Then he would grab two hours' sleep on the couch in the basement, shower, dress, and head off to the hospital for his morning rounds.

When he was in the basement, he locked the door, with a DO NOT DISTURB sign nailed up in case the locked door was not clear enough.

Technically this man was home every moment he was not at work, but Theodora tearfully told me that days would go by when she literally would not speak to or see him. Their kids had even nicknamed him "the Invisible Man." He was living a separate life in his well-furnished hermit cave.

At my suggestion Theodora insisted on having a face-to-face discussion with him about the problem. She told me that when she went to his office and sat across from him, he looked anxious and his knees pumped up and down as if he was trying to run away while sitting there. She felt that he could hardly wait for her to leave, and she was right on target about this. After she said a few things, he locked the door behind her as she left, and went back to his computer life.

I wish I had a happy ending to relate to you concerning Theodora and her husband. I never saw her again and have no idea if anything changed between them. The gift I got from her was to become much more aware of modern techno-hermits. People do not need to physically go off somewhere to emotionally check out. They can be there in body, but not in mind or spirit. Now, don't misunderstand me, I love my computer, e-mail my friends on it, eBay on it, and write my books on it. But I also know that there have been many times that I look at the clock and four hours have slipped by without my knowing it, and not in a productive way. The computer habit is a way to fall down a socially acceptable rabbit hole into virtual hermit behavior.

If you are a hermit or married to one, you need to establish face time. It doesn't matter whether you are watching porn or reading the classics on the computer (okay, maybe a little); the point is that while you may be having a rollicking good time online, hobnobbing with busty cartoon girls or with six-headed armed robots, or reading a blog about someone's thoughts on the proper clipping of toenails, you are sitting in a chair, staring into a screen, and typing. This is not real life. You need to reacquaint yourself with the sound, smell, and touch of human beings. The name for people who have trouble with this has changed over the years: grumpy old men, isolators, shy people, wallflowers, social phobics, and inner-directed, to name a few. As the world gets more hectic, crowded, and disturbing, it may seem like the best solution is to stay in your room and live a virtual life. But even the English hermit living on the lord's estate was expected to be available from time to time to talk with his master.

THE WHEEL OF FORTUNE

THE WHEEL OF FORTUNE

CARD NUMBER 10

The wheel of fortune turns round incessantly, and who can say to himself, I shall today be uppermost.

—CONFUCIUS

At this point in his life journey, the Fool has just come from the enforced downtime required by the Hermit card. He has learned about caution and prudence and is now ready to move forward. The Wheel of Fortune is a very lucky card, but it does not guarantee anything. It is the go-ahead-take-a-chance card. If you get this card placed right-side up and dead center in a reading, buy a lottery ticket or go to the casino. If you are starting a new endeavor, this is the marker card you will be happy to see. It is a big green light.

One thing I have often seen in my readings is how people miss the cues to start an endeavor. Let me tell you about Emily Anne, a nice young woman who seemed to be color-blind when it came to seeing the green light ahead. As the reading commenced I shuffled the cards, she shuffled the cards, and we jumped into the deep end of the pool to answer two questions that felt monumental to her. The first was whether she should marry her boyfriend of many years; the second if she should stay at her job or look for another. The Wheel of Fortune came up in both readings, along with Minor Arcana cards that underscored the positive reasons to both marry her boyfriend and look for another job. It could not have been more clear to me that the answer was yes on both counts.

I love it when the cards make my work easy. With a big smile I told Emily Anne that she should marry and get a new job. She looked at me as if I were speaking Esperanto. I said it again, wondering if I was mumbling, but she still did not seem to understand me.

"So I am not sure what I should do about my boyfriend," she said with her forehead all scrunched up. Again I repeated that the cards were all in favor of the marriage. She sat with this for a few minutes and then said, "And what about a job." I wondered if she had a hearing problem that I had not realized. Loudly I said, "Emily Anne, the cards are saying very definitely that you should marry your boyfriend and look for a better job."

"Oh," she said flatly.

Time passed as I let this sink in.

"Is there anything else you would like to know?" I said.

"Well . . . I just do not know what I should do about marrying Tim."

"What about the job?" I queried.

"I need some direction with both of those things," Emily Anne said.

And again we were at the beginning.

Have you ever sat in the driver's seat of a car, pressing the gas pedal after accidentally having placed the gearshift in neutral? You assume something dire must be wrong with the car, and then you realize it is not the car but you who has caused this problem. A wheeled vehicle that is sitting still is of no use to anyone. The Wheel of Fortune card is similar: When stalled it does no good.

If tarot cards were judged on their mythic content, then the Wheel of Fortune would win hands down. Wheels have been discussed and dissected from biblical times forward. Ezekiel saw a wheel within a wheel in the sky. The wheels "sparkled like chrysolite and all four looked alike. Each appeared to be made like a wheel intersecting a wheel" (Ezekiel 1:16). Buddhist mandalas are shaped like wheels, crop circles are wheels, ring-around-the-rosy is a wheel, when we get married we place a circular ring on our finger. Even Stephen Hawkins (who sits in a wheelchair) said: "All the evidence shows that God was actually quite a gambler, and the universe is a great casino, where dice are thrown, and roulette wheels spin on every occasion."

When we go to a casino, we hope for a big payoff, and this is also what the Fool craves. Remember, there is no promise of victory, so while he may win big, he may also lose. But at least he is still in the game, and that is about as much of a pledge as life will give any of us.

The tarot demands from us balance in all things, and why should the Wheel of Fortune be any different? I have a friend who is a wealthy woman and a compulsive gambler. This might sound glamorous, bringing up images of Monte Carlo high life and baccarat tournaments, but my friend's idea of a good time is to go to Atlantic City, buy herself a huge cardboard tub of nickels, and sit all day at a slot machine feeding it her change.

If you have ever been to a casino, you may have noticed that they are cleverly designed to edit out your ability to tell day from night. There are no clocks, and they are designed to skew your innate sense of direction. You can wander around a casino and lose your way; everything is equally bright and noisy and intense. What the Fool is called upon to do with this card is to keep his bearings and find a path through the noisy ruckus. He may partake of the fun and the possibility of riches, but he must keep moving or he will wind up sitting in front of the metaphorical slot machine for all eternity. He will continue to pull the handle and never win anything big.

Many years back I had a client who was a truly lovely woman as well as a gifted musician. She was forever experiencing financial and emotional hard times when she should have been at the top of her profession with accolades pouring in from all over. Here is how she had stopped the Wheel of Fortune from rolling forward on her behalf:

Betsy had been with a small city orchestra since she left Juilliard. Her teachers there assumed that she would be playing with a major company, but she was too shy and unassertive to try for those positions. She liked being the big fish in a small pond because no one expected more from her than she'd originally come with. She was very good, and very good she would stay. There was no reason to strive for excellence because she was fine the way she was—or so she thought until another woman who played for the same small orchestra was offered a job with a more prestigious orchestra in a big city. She was not as talented as Betsy and her training was nowhere near as good. To look at both Betsy and this other woman from the outside was to see two demure musicians, their hair tucked behind velvet headbands, garbed in similar long black skirts and white silk blouses. They appeared a matched set—except that the less talented musician was always looking for a way up and out of the small-town orchestra, while Betsy clung to it.

Betsy was less a barnacle than the proverbial ostrich with its head buried in the sand (which apparently ostriches in real life do not do, but it is still a great image). She missed all the opportunities the other woman grabbed. During our reading she acted like the other woman had been miraculously snatched up by fate and plunked down in a chair of this important orchestra. I tried to get Betsy to calm down enough to deconstruct what really happened. There was no magic involved, just the usual open doors that people who succeed wiggle their way through.

Betsy's rival had made repeated visits to the city where the prestigious orchestra played. She crashed parties given in their honor and charmed the people who made hiring decisions. She kept in touch with them with notes and little gifts, she sent tapes of herself playing and asked important musicians whom she had met to write letters of recommendation for her, which she in turn sent on to the head of the other orchestra. Meanwhile Betsy bought new velvet headbands and dutifully showed up for work every day. She was a wonderful musician but socially invisible. She had put a boot on the Wheel of Fortune, and it was stuck in place.

While we were discussing this, Betsy came up with the most amazing and most un-Betsy-like comment: "If I picture an ostrich with its head in the sand, what does another meaner and more predatory ostrich see?" she mused. I had no idea where she was going with this, but I let her continue. "If I was an aggressive ostrich looking to conquer and I saw another ostrich with its head in the sand, I would also see a big unguarded ostrich ass sticking up in the air, just ready to be f*cked over." I almost fell off my chair when these words came from Betsy's dainty mouth.

But boy was she right, and I had never heard it explained quite so succinctly. It is not just that the first ostrich had blinded itself from seeing; it also positioned itself for any marauding ostriches that came ambling by to have their way with it.

Betsy was a quick learner. She pulled her head out of the sand and realized that she deserved a better job. Going nowhere had at first felt comforting and secure, but now it seemed unbearable and a waste of time.

While she did not have great schmoozing skills, she did have talent. So she too sent tapes and letters to orchestras she wanted to be a part of and made herself highly visible and available to offers. Soon an offer came through, and Betsy was very excited. The last time we met face-to-face (the new job was across the country), she informed me that it was going to be just another stepping-stone in her career, not the end of the path.

If I needed to name one problem that most people who come to me for a reading share, it would be their inability to move ahead. There is a big difference between moving on and running away. People who run away from their problems always find the same issue at their new address, wrapped up in a shiny red bow waiting at their front door. The saying "No matter where you go, there you are" is true. To move ahead you have to figure out why you got into the situation to begin with. I will be the first to agree that this is hard work, maybe the hardest work you will ever have to do, but when the old patterns fall away and the new horizon appears you will be happy you persevered.

JUSTICE

JUSTICE

CARD NUMBER 11

Look at the judge, a guy who spends half his life in school. He's a lawyer, and then he's a lower judge, then an upper judge. He works his way up to some big important murder trial like this, and he doesn't even get to decide if the guy is guilty or not. No, that decision's made by five salesmen, three plumbers, two bank tellers, and a dingbat.

—ARCHIE BUNKER

Bob, an otherwise nice man and a sometime client of mine, has been stuck on the meaning of the Justice card for way too long. If I were less professional as a reader, I would have screamed at him to wake up and smell the coffee. It is uncanny how often he draws the card in a reading and how he always manages to deny what it's about.

The Justice card can be very satisfying or, as in Bob's case, a stumbling block to self-actualization. Justice is just what it sounds like: It is about being fair and having people be equally fair with you. It concerns doing the right thing no matter what the occasion and speaking the truth even if it is personally painful. It is, in the parlance of twelve-step programs, about making a fearless moral inventory and then making amends to those you have hurt.

Here is Bob on the Justice card:

"I don't know why I cough all the time." (Bob smokes three packs a day.)

"I don't know why my wife thinks I don't love her." (Bob forgets her birthday, forgets their anniversary, and eats his dinner in front of the blaring TV.)

"I should have gotten that promotion at work." (Bob's boss caught him leaving for a fishing trip when he called in sick.)

"I can't make ends meet on my salary." (Bob recently bought a new boat, a home entertainment center, and a Rolex.)

By now you want to smack him upside the head too, don't you?

The Justice card is about cause and effect. You do this and that happens. You eat too much and you gain weight, you kick a dog and it bites you, you are obnoxious and people don't like you. Not really a hard formula, but one that a surprising number of people cannot grasp. Denial is how the Bobs of the world operate, and being able to not understand how your actions relate to your life is a major stumbling block.

It is very human to blame others for your faults. I remember being ten years old, an only child, and telling my mother that another kid broke the living room lamp, took money from her purse, and ate all the cookies. Exactly who this naughty child was and how she got into our apartment never occurred to me; I was just too hell-bent on having the blame shifted onto another for logic to intrude. Did this silly behavior stop for me at age ten? Of course not. Like almost everyone else I told teachers the dog ate my homework, told police I was speeding because of an emergency at home, and feigned innocent horror when my husband asked how the Visa bill had grown so large. My inner Bob was always tempting me to blame someone else for my situations.

The bottom line is that we fool nobody but ourselves when we act this way. People see right through us most of the time. Our faces and body language sometimes give us away, but more often we set off other people's inner bullshit detectors by what we do and say.

Now, here is where the Justice card gets tricky.

The heart and soul of the Justice card is the hard truth that life is not fair. Wonderful people die too young, O. J. Simpson is found not guilty, Bernie Madoff steals his friends' money, the best horse loses the race, a nun gets raped, a man cheats on his lovely wife with her best friend, and the most annoying song in the world tops the charts. There is not a day that goes by that I, you, or we do not shake our heads in dismay. How could they, what were they thinking, it's unfair, she didn't deserve that, I just do not get it. It takes a ton of maturity to know that things often do not happen the way they should. We get so angry that we lose faith in God. We lose faith in our fellow man, and eventually we lose faith in ourselves as well. We feel it doesn't matter if we cheat a little or lie a little or steal a little; everyone does it, don't they?

For the Fool on his life's journey, Justice is another seemingly insurmountable obstacle to climb. It is now time for truth and honesty, accepting cause and effect, and making hard decisions. The Fool has just passed through the Wheel of Fortune, his personal crossroads or turning point. He has been forced to make a decision between option A and option B, and having committed to one or the other he now must accept the rewards or fallout from his actions.

This is card number eleven; he is halfway though his journey. The Fool, to use modern parlance, is having his midlife crisis. At this point making changes is not easy, no matter what we do. Even if it is right for us, a change may cause distress and anger. It is time to set things right, to offer apologies, to explain ourselves and our actions, and to try to remedy any pain and suffering we have caused others. This is a significant maturing process in our lives, because we are forced to see the ripples caused by what we do, and to know that what seems unfair to us may seem perfectly fair to someone else.

———•———

In the image at the start of this chapter, taken from the Bohemian Gothic Tarot deck, the figure in the Justice card is a stern-looking judge, exactly like the image you will see in a courthouse, except here Justice is not blindfolded. With a cold eye the figure looks right at you and decides right from wrong.

{ 102 }

When I draw the Justice card for a client, my first question is always "Are you involved in any lawsuits or legal actions?" Nine out of ten times I get no as a response. Then as the reading unravels, I hear about the contentious divorce, the rewriting of a will, the liens on the house, and a score of other things that for some strange reason the client does not immediately see as involving the law. I think this is an offshoot of television. Unless the situation looks like an episode of *Law and Order,* or someone is being dragged in handcuffs out of the house as they do in *Cops,* people do not think of the high drama in their lives as falling under the banner of the law. To them Justice implies criminal behavior, so if you are reading for someone, make it very clear that you are not implying he's a felon.

Some readers believe that the Justice card is dealt reversed when it relates literally to the law. I don't think it matters if the thing is reversed, right-side up, or tipped sideways—somehow it will involve a third person making a decision about who is right and who is wrong. It need not be a judge in a courthouse; it could be a boss or a supervisor, or even your tax auditor. Someone, somewhere is about to rule on some aspect of your life.

A slightly more subtle approach to reading this card is as a warning of being too judgemental. I do not mean judging right from wrong, which is pretty clear-cut in our society. From the Ten Commandments to local statutes, most things we do have a thumbs-up or thumbs-down rule: You must not kill people, you can't steal, you must get your dog a yearly license, you must not sashay around naked outside your house—that sort of thing. The kind of behavior I am referring to is not bound by the law but involves snubbing your nose at other people through prejudice, bigotry, or a sense of entitlement. There may not be an official sanction regarding this mean behavior, but the universe is noticing what you do and I can promise you that sometime, someplace, somehow, you will be called to task for it.

There is often some confusion between the Justice card and the Judgement card, as both inhabit the same territory: being called on your actions. However, the Justice card is not a subtle card; it can be very black and white, and can literally relate to legal things. When it shows itself in my readings, "maybe" is usually not the answer. Justice does not give readers much wiggle room to dance away from a question they may be too squeamish to answer bluntly. Ultimately as the reader you need to tell the client the truth, but you may also need to soften the blow a bit to make the truth palatable. Questions like "Is my husband filing for a divorce" from a weepy wife, or "Is my mother going to leave her fortune to my other sister" coming from a lady with five children who is trying hard to make ends meet, are not fun to answer unless the outcome is what the client hopes to hear. The Justice card is one of those that does not speak in metaphors. A jail sentence is not a metaphor, collecting alimony is not a metaphor, and being sued is not a metaphor. When a judge hits his gavel and makes a proclamation, he is not going to phrase the sentence as "You may at some point in your life find that money is not going to come your way." He will say whatever he has to say bluntly: "You are fined $5,000," or "Your mother has left everything in her will to your sister." After the verdict the judge retires to chambers, letting the distraught plaintiff deal with things. As a reader I do not have a chamber to disappear to; I break clients' hearts and then have to sit at the table with them watching the news take its toll. This is when I do not like reading cards one bit.

THE HANGED MAN

THE HANGED MAN

CARD NUMBER 12

Go instead where there is no path and leave a trail.

—ANONYMOUS

The Hanged Man is one of the strangest looking of the Major Arcana cards. The card shows a figure nailed upside down. He is not struggling (as you or I certainly would do in this position), nor does he look happy. He just dangles there like a deflated wind sock.

The image of the hanged man has been interpreted over the years with much religious symbolism. The figure on the card looks like an upside-down crucified Christ, and also mirrors the myth of Odin, the Norse god who hung upside down from the World Tree until he achieved wisdom. In many decks the figure of this man bears a halo, which radiates from his head, another valid reason to look on him as a holy man.

Despite its veil of religiousness, I read this card in a very basic manner, since what Odin did, or even Christ's travails, is too far removed from my clients' modern-day of-the-moment predicaments. When people are in crisis, they are often put off by folktales or myths. When your husband runs off with your best friend, do you really care what Aesop said?

I put my own spin on this card (a squeamish pun when you are dealing with a tarot figure that looks like a whirligig), as I often do with others. I have always believed that a reader has every right to make her own interpretation of a card, as long as she stays within the parameters of its classic meaning. It would be a strange tarot reader who explained the Hanged Man as a symbol of a Trans Am muscle car, or an eggplant Parmesan sandwich.

With this said, I very prosaically use the Hanged Man in my readings as a sign that people are "hung up," that they can't move forward or make up their mind about whatever it is that they must decide on. When clients draw the Hanged Man, I start to ask them what they are on the fence about. If I am lucky they will tell me right away, but at other times the discussion proceeds as follows:

JANE: What are you hung up about?

CLIENT: I can't decide if I should live in France or Italy.

(Much time passes as the client explains the positive and negative side of each country to me.)

CLIENT: So where should I live?

JANE: I don't know, you tell me.

CLIENT: I don't know.

And on it goes, spinning like a wheel but going nowhere. Of course people get hung up on important things (who to marry, where to live), and on silly things as well (the color of a dress or serving potatoes versus rice). If you find decision making easy, then you will not fall into mulling things over until they lose all meaning and sense.

As a reader I can only hear so much of this endless waffling before falling into the trap of attempting to decide for the client. I used to do this frequently, but I don't do it much anymore because it doesn't work. If a client asked me where he should live and I said "Italy," I would get bombarded with a dozen reasons why France is better. If I said "France" my client would suddenly divulge a great love for Vespas and Chianti. You can't win with this shortcut, because the payoff is not that the client gets a decision made by an impartial party, it's that he has enticed you into his worrisome vortex, and believe me when I say you are not alone. People who claim to not be able to decide have armies of eager volunteer helpers surrounding them.

It is very seductive and flattering for know-it-alls like me to be asked to make important decisions for someone else. The problem comes when you realize that your well-considered words of wisdom have been tossed on the floor like shelled peanuts at a bar. In rapid order, here is what happens with "poll taking" friends and relatives and why you should not engage:

Five Easy Steps for People Who Want Other People to Decide for Them

STEP ONE: In excruciating detail, lay out the situation you are unable to make a decision about. Explain all the pluses and minuses to the sympathetic ear listening to you. Spare no detail, no matter how small or boring: Make sure your listener knows Aunt Mildred is married to Uncle Leo's ex-boss, and that Judy is allergic to seafood.

STEP TWO: After a thorough explanation of the situation, appear to listen to your friends' thoughtful reasoning, nod and look pensive, but secretly immediately disregard it.

STEP THREE: When you see them the next time (and of course you have still not made a decision), launch into the whole saga again, imploring them to help you.

STEP FOUR: Watch them run screaming away from you into the night.

STEP FIVE: Find another kindly, good-intentioned soul and begin the process again.

———•———

There is a show on TV that I am fascinated with because it shows a full spectrum of decision making. *Say Yes to the Dress* takes place at Kleinfeld bridal store in Manhattan. The show has a very simple premise: Brides go to this store to try on wedding dresses and buy the one they like best. Kleinfeld has thousands of bridal dresses in stock, and they all basically look the same: white, long, and decorated with pretty trimmings. The riveting thing is to see how bride after bride approaches the task of selecting the right dress.

Many brides try on three or four dresses before they commit. Others try on two dozen and need the entourage they brought with them to help them decide. And then there are a few who would like to try on every dress in the store, nitpick and complain, and after hours and hours leave empty-handed because they just can't decide. They have driven the sales staff crazy and caused this viewer to yell *"Pick one!"* loudly at the screen, but they do not seem to hear me.

The Hanged Man right-side up can be the mark of a connoisseur, someone whose taste level is above the commonplace and—using great discernment—picks wisely. The Hanged Man right-side up also refers to someone who uses all five senses and even extrasensory perception to make a decision. People who fall into this category can be difficult to please, not because they are clueless and needy but because their image of what they want has yet to materialize. You can often tell these people from their indecisive counterparts by their swiftness in saying no. Give connoisseurs a stack of anything and they will go through it at lightning speed, discarding the dross looking for the gold. In the same scenario, the hopelessly confused have a deer-in-the-headlights look about them. They might rustle through the stack a bit, but will then break down and cry and ask a friend what they think.

Clients who have a hard time decision making are often terribly insecure about themselves. Here is a snippet of dialogue in a conversation I had with a woman named Emma, who is a very timid soul.

JANE: Have you read any good books lately?

EMMA: I read the one that was number one on the *New York Times* best-seller list.

JANE: Did you like it?

EMMA: Not really, but I must be wrong because it is a best seller.

Emma only goes to restaurants that have had great write-ups, only attends movies that critics gave thumbs-up to, and only buys clothing she has seen on celebrities. She is a label queen; no matter how hideously ugly a handbag may be, if it is a Gucci or a Vuitton it is safe to buy because it is from a designer and no one will question her taste. The funny thing is that Emma is not at all a snob, but she is terrified that she might make a misstep so she goes by what the tastemakers say is in or out.

If you have never been in a surging crowd, consider yourself lucky. Crowds surge for any number of reasons, from political rallies, to soccer matches, to Black Friday at the mall. On these occasions, crowds can take on a life of their own; people mesh into a giant wave of humanity that gobbles up everything in front of it. This juggernaut is blind, deaf, and senseless, unlike the individual people in it.

If you let "the crowd" push you ahead instead of using your own taste and logic, you will often be swept into a bad place or left trampled underfoot. One of the things that makes human beings human is that we have the power to reason. We are not a herd of stampeding elephants or lemmings about to fling ourselves off a cliff. We have the capacity to analyze situations and make informed decisions. If you draw the Hanged Man reversed, it might be a good time to figure out where you begin and the crowd ends.

———•———

This brings us to the final definition of this card: self-sacrifice and purification. If you ever travel in India, you will see Holy

Men who are seeking to get in touch with the divine by doing any number of odd things. Some hold one arm up in the air for twenty years, others claim never to eat, and some dangle upside down from a tree like the Hanged Man himself. When a client draws this card and I find she is not struggling with an inability to make a choice or being too caught up in group thinking, I explore whether she's just overloaded with possessions and needs to pare things down. Many of us swing back and forth between buying things and getting rid of them. We stuff and purge ourselves with possessions, drastically daydreaming of an item and then wanting it out of the house. Have you been to a Goodwill Superstore lately? It is like Neiman Marcus; the quality of other people's junk has been raised beyond measure. Among the most lucrative businesses are those that haul away stuff we no longer want or rent us storage facilities to house stuff we don't want but are too uncertain to get rid of. Drawing the Hanged Man card may be a mandate to streamline your living situation. Cleaning out the clutter is good for the soul as well as the eye. If cluttering is your problem, it is very likely you will draw this card.

Like anything else in life, you de-clutter one thing at a time. Can you live with 299 pairs of high heels instead of 300? Do you really need every issue of *Time* magazine even though it is available online? Some people hang on to belongings because they do not want to be wasteful; others attach sentiments to things and cannot imagine being able to call up that feeling if the object is not there. Letting go is easy for some and almost impossible for others, but if you are able to accomplish this task it will clear your energy field and you will find yourself less distracted.

DEATH

DEATH

For death begins with life's first breath and life begins at touch of death.

—JOHN OXENHAM, ENGLISH POET

The Death card is perhaps the most dramatic card in the deck. I am referring to the reaction from the other side of the table when I place it in a layout. Only those well versed in tarot accept it as meaning the end of something, or of making way for new beginnings. Most people simply freak out. In my years as a reader, I have seen the full gamut of emotions, from a slight pallor or a tiny tremor in the hands, to full Get Me The Hell Out Of Here reactions that have included knocking the table (and me) over and running out my front door as fast as possible.

Unless you are a Goth, death is scary, and nobody much likes to see that gruesome skeleton grinning up from the unfurled deck. At that point it is tempting for the reader to do a song and dance about how the Death card is not really about death, but I am a Scorpio, having six planets in the sign of the zodiac ruled by death, and I am possibly the only person whose shrink once compared her to Darth Vader. I am too old to be walking around in black lipstick and piercings, but to be honest I do have a dark side and occasionally have a wallow in it.

By dark side I do not mean evil, but I seem to be on awfully chummy terms with death. Before I turned twenty-five my mother and father died, my two same-age cousins died, my grandmother died, my uncle died, my aunt died, and my dog died. I am sure I am leaving someone out of this gloomy roster because after the umpteenth call telling me when the funeral was, I kind of blanked out and lost track. As an only child, being without kin was not easy. Back then I knew no one my age who had ever lost anything more meaningful than a pet hamster. So, following my natural Scorpio traits, I morphed into a sullen, angry presence and took to wearing a ragged black coat from the Salvation Army store, in case anyone failed to notice I was grieving. In my mourning dress, with my center-parted ink-black hair, I was a prototype for Professor Snape of Harry Potter.

But let's get back to the tarot deck—as soon as I tell you one unsettling story. About ten years ago I was doing a reading for a nice suburban mom of three. I went to her house, which looked both clean and comfy. She had baked oatmeal raisin cookies for the kids when they came home from school.

There was absolutely nothing amiss with the picture of this happy home, but when we started the reading and I did layout after layout, the Death card popped up front and center in every hand. I began to get a very creepy feeling, and not only because the Death card did not seem to have a relevant context in her happy home. I asked if anyone she knew was ill, but the answer was no. I don't think I have ever done such an elaborate tap dance around the Death card as I did that day. I reached for the safe and possibly optimistic "end of a phase of your life" business, to which she looked at me with confusion. "What's ending?" she asked. I had no idea and neither did she. I was almost ready to lie and tell her there were twenty or more Death cards in the deck (to explain why it kept coming up), but instead I stuffed an oatmeal cookie in my mouth and smiled weakly.

I was glad when the hour ended. I felt that I had told her a bunch of gobbledygook. I was too proud to admit I had no idea why that card kept coming up, but I could not stand the thought of scaring this sweet, upbeat lady. Of course this story has an unhappy ending. An hour after I left her house her healthy, handsome, thirty-five-year-old stock-broker husband dropped dead from an aneurism at work. I found out about it the next day in the local newspaper obits. This event changed her life, and it spooked me deeply. What should I have done? Could I have alerted her and possibly intervened in some meaningful way? I suspect that a hysterical wife's phone call to a brokerage house to tell her husband that a tarot card reader said he or someone close to her was about to drop dead would not have been met with much concern.

So yes, the Death card can be literal (you die) or metaphorical (you end something, divest yourself of aspects of your personality, and make way for a new you). One thing to consider when confronted with the Death card is that it is not the last Major Arcana card in the deck. It comes somewhere in the middle of the Fool's journey, and thus implies that death is not necessarily final, but a transition we all must make. Fortunately the Death card is largely metaphorical or symbolic. I would not read cards if every time that card hit the table, the client (or someone close to her) was literally going to die. I couldn't take it. I do not think I have ever met a serious reader who likes to be the bearer of bad news.

But let's stick with the Death card when it literally means death is approaching. Since the cards are influenced by the cards around them in a spread, when Death is dealt I look to see what the full message is. Are the cards talking about poor health, or health issues that the client can control, like smoking or drugs? Is there travel in the reading; if so, is there a danger from a plane or car, and can the card be given as a warning to heed? Does the Death card indicate impending violence, surgery that should be postponed, or suicide? Yes, it can mean all of the above.

One of my most memorable readings was with a client who had an abusive boyfriend. He beat her up, he threatened her, and he was in general a seriously scary guy. Her reading was consistently about death and violence. I warned her to kick him out and get a restraining order, a security alarm, a mean dog—whatever it would take to keep safe. As with most abused women, she was so deep into her morass that although she nodded to me as we talked, I could tell nothing was going to change. One night around 10:00 p.m. I was in bed, propped by pillows, reading a good book when the phone rang. I try to not take calls at that hour but intuitively I picked up the phone this time and heard her voice. "He just broke into the house and he has a gun, what do the cards think I should do?" I bolted upright. "Run out of the house and call the police," I yelled at her. Ladies and gentlemen, there are times when you do not need cards to tell you what to do next. I saw this woman a few weeks later. She had a black eye and a swollen lip. I assumed the boyfriend was now in jail, but no, she'd refused to press charges and everything was back the way it was. I stopped working with her because I knew that the Death card would now not mean big changes, but a foretelling of her demise, and there was nothing I could do to help her.

You might be interested in hearing about those clients I mentioned earlier, the ones who ran out the door when card number thirteen hit the table. Scott was a stockbroker from a posh town for whom the Death card translated as a man who would soon lose his job, a major end of a way of being. Scott was a walking billboard for status, from the designer cashmere sweaters he slung around his neck, to his yacht club affiliation, to the Bentley he drove. To be without his things was, for Scott, a fate worse than death, and he could not stand to hear that from me. He called a month later, after he had been sacked from the job, lost his trophy girlfriend, and was now wearing nondesigner jeans. Amazingly he was bright and happy. He had lost everything he thought defined him, and to his utter surprise was beginning to find the previously unknown Scott who did not have his future so neatly in place. Although the door had shut behind him, he was getting used to waiting in the proverbial hallway until the next door opened; in fact he was rather enjoying it. Since the Death card is about fear of the unknown, once Scott's eyes became used to the darkness he relaxed and like a cave adventurer began to see the beauty in it.

I heard from Scott a year later. He called and told me he had chucked it all and become a cheese maker in Oregon. When he heard my shocked silence on the other end of the phone, he laughed and said he was kidding and had in fact found another job at another prestigious brokerage firm and everything was fine. I asked him if he went back to his girlfriend and if he still had the Bentley and he said, "No, that's not really me anymore." In my mind I pictured the Death card looking rather carefree, even with a cashmere sweater wrapped jauntily around its shoulders, preppy-style. Like the body when a person dies, death strips you clean down to the bones. The Death card is about cutting out the extraneous in your life, and Scott had done just that. He had filled his life up with so many things that he had lost sight of the essential structure that supported it.

There are of course many views on Death, and the way you think about it is indeed culturally influenced. I am almost sure that my neighbor in suburban Connecticut thinks differently about Death than a street beggar in Bangladesh. If you boil down the messages of most of the world's religions and philosophies about Death, it is a rather short menu:

Death is the end; you die and that is all there is.

Death is the beginning of yet another reincarnation or transformation.

Death means you go to heaven, purgatory, or hell.

There are no such places; the only place you go after death is into the grave.

The soul and your energy survive after death.

Nothing survives death, you become worm food.

After death you are reunited with your deceased loved ones.

It is all a big black nothing. There is no afterlife.

It is an eternal debate and I will not begin to address which path you should choose, except to say that personally I have had more than enough strange experiences to doubt that the spirit ceases to exist after death.

I do not go ghost hunting, but I did once see a ghost. When I was thirteen years old (coincidentally the number of the Death card), my parents moved into a luxurious apartment on the Upper East Side of Manhattan. The first night in my new bedroom, I fell asleep and a short while later awoke to see a luminescent figure sitting in a chair next to the bed. My first thought was terror, but very quickly I felt a great sense of peace wash over me and fell back to sleep. In the morning I chalked it up to a nutty dream, one that I shared with my mother. She then told me that the apartment had come on the market because the lady who lived there had died, in my bedroom. Instead of making me never want to revisit that room again, the apparition made sense to me; she was a benign ghost just curious about who had moved in, and once she saw the new family (and me), she moved on.

Being a tarot reader herself, my mother had common ground with ghosts. When her father died in California (3,000 miles away), our electric kitchen clock stopped at the moment of his death and all the china fell out of the kitchen cabinets. When her father-in-law died and the family members congregated at his apartment on the top floor of the Mayflower Hotel overlooking Central Park, a huge colorful macaw flew in through the open window, did a few laps around the apartment, and flew back out. The deceased had been a lifelong parrot fancier, but a South American macaw coming in the window was startling. A pigeon maybe, but a macaw in Midtown Manhattan?

The Death card is indeed dramatic. It figures in Bizet's opera *Carmen,* when in the third act Carmen draws this card and shortly after dies. The Beltway Snipers who terrified Washington, DC, in 2007 by randomly shooting at strangers left the Death card at their crime scenes for the FBI to find.

Let's take another look at the symbolism of the Death card. It is (to say the least) weird and confusing. In fact, the only thing clear about this card from deck to deck is that it makes our toes curl. The classic image of the Death card can be seen on the Rider-Waite deck, featuring a skeleton wearing a suit of armor on horseback (Death himself). But what's with the dead king wearing an ermine robe, lying on his back with his crown on the ground? Who's the bishop to the right, with his hands raised in prayer? What are we to make of the two figures with crowns of flowers on their heads? On the horizon the sun either sets or rises over two castle towers (some say the skyline of New Jerusalem or the mountains of the moon). Huh? Oddly, most people who sit across the table from me are so transfixed by the Grim Reaper that they never notice the other cast of characters on the card. Let me see if I can explain these elements to you.

The dead king signifies the unstoppable majesty of Death. It conquers all men in the end, and is a great equalizer. The flag that the skeleton carries is black with a white rose on it. Symbolically a white rose is mystical shorthand for the cycle of death and rebirth. The bishop, unlike the king, is still standing and is meant to show that the only thing as powerful as Death is faith. The two flower-bedecked people are meant to be a mother and child or a young person and an old person. The older of the pair looks over her shoulder with the great grief that accompanies Death. The child, more inno-cent, looks straight-on at the figure on the horse, less with fear than with curiosity.

Not all tarot decks have this image. The illustration at the start of this chapter shows the Death card from the wonder-fully macabre Bohemian Gothic deck. Here a skeleton stands with a regal red sash on his bony shoulders, and he presides over a mass of horizontal skeletons at his feet. Every tarot artist's interpretation of the Death card is wildly different. In some a skeleton rides a horse, in others he walks wield-ing a scythe. In some decks he wears a helmet with red rib-bons; in others he wears the crown of Osiris, the Egyptian god of the dead. Not all images on the Death card show the king or the bishop—some decks have an onion, a snake, a fish, a scorpion, or a lily, all symbolic in their own way. In the Rider-Waite deck, Death looks rather nice. He is smiling broadly (easy for a skull to do); his horse is plump and clean and decked out with a handsome bridle and reins. He looks like something you might see in the Rose Bowl parade, until you realize, *Oh yes, that's not Roy Rogers on Trigger, it's Death.*

These strange tableaus are meant to depict all the mixed emotions that accompany death, either metaphorical or lit-eral. No one escapes death; no one even escapes the ups and downs of life that shock us from our complacency.

This is the point of the Death card. No matter what deck you use, and no matter what the graphic image is, it is meant to look frightening. But the longer you look at it, the less scary and, in many ways, the more mysteriously beautiful it becomes. The card truly demystifies death. Death is just part of the landscape. People fall, they get up; they fall from grace, they are reborn with a set of fresh and innocent eyes; and as Death's horse's hooves hit the earth, the journey continues over and over again without end. Every culture has a symbol for death and rebirth, and for many who read the tarot, this is ours.

TEMPERANCE

TEMPERANCE

CARD NUMBER 14

The science of alchymy I like very well, and indeed, 'tis the philosophy of the ancients. I like it not only for the profits it brings in melting metals, in decocting, preparing, extracting and distilling herbs, roots; I like it also for the sake of the allegory and secret signification, which is exceedingly fine, touching the resurrection of the dead at the last day.

—MARTIN LUTHER, *TABLE TALK*

What a neighborhood this Major Arcana card lives in: smack between Death and the Devil—*quelle horreur!* At the midpoint of his journey, the Fool takes on the aspect of the protagonist of a horror movie who thinks he is on safe ground, only to discover he is still in the middle of a nightmare.

The Temperance card is notoriously hard to read. It seems at the very least a mass of contradictions. This card is about moderation, not letting yourself get swept away in a riptide of manic behavior, where too much seems just about right. To modern folk, the very word *temperance* has a Carrie Nation feel about it, a starchy look down the nose at anyone who imbibes or overindulges. Nowadays few people remember the Temperance Movement at the turn of the twentieth century, when scores of sober-sided ladies and a few prissy men appeared at bars and taverns across the land, armed with axes and hatchets, and smashed these places of ill repute to splinters. "Demon rum" and other alcoholic beverages were seen as the work of the devil, luring men away from their families and jobs and into the gutters of dereliction. One reading of this tarot card harks back to this old-fashioned philosophy of abstinence. But the Temperance card is not just about sobriety in regard to alcohol, it demands from the Fool moderation in all his endeavors. The Fool is now mature, and binges and wild indulgences are no longer acceptable.

In most decks this card shows a large angel holding two goblets, mixing the contents. No, the angel is not a bartender, and the contents of the two goblets are not the makings of a dirty martini. They are symbolic of the different streams of life that must be blended in equal proportions to make us mature. The angel mixing this soul cocktail has a look of great tranquility on her face. She is usually shown between vines and fishes. Fish are an ancient symbol for creativity, and vines symbolize growth. This optimistic rendering complements the fact that the astrological sign Sagittarius rules this card. Sagittarius is an expansive sign full of adventure and a love for excitement.

I have a number of clients who are recovering alcoholics, and the Temperance card loves to pop up throughout their readings. There is always an awkward moment in working with a new client when Temperance is the central card in a layout and I ask him point-blank if he's an alcoholic—only those comfortably in recovery will admit to this. If he himself isn't burdened with this problem, a spouse or family member likely is. Often clients will say they like a few glasses of wine after work, or a beer on the weekend, when the few glasses are in fact two bottles, and the beer is usually twelve cans. Please do not get me wrong. I drink (to me, there is nothing better at the end of the day then a gin and tonic), but having lived with an alcoholic I know the difference between normal and abnormal drinking. I am not talking about social drinking here.

Leaving alcoholism to one side, the Temperance card has also been very active in my readings for a whole new class of intemperate people, specifically shopaholics. I recently read that shopping is America's number one pastime. Megamalls, discount stores, coupons, and home shopping networks on TV make it too easy to spend money you probably do not have to squander. Many people I read for literally cannot pass a store with a SALE sign in the window without parking their car; the words 50 PERCENT OFF are like crack. I have clients who are addicted to Cartier, I have clients addicted to thrift shops and tag sales, and it makes no difference because their compulsions are at the core the same.

It really is perfect that the Temperance card sits in the deck between Death and the Devil. Overindulgence in food, shopping, booze, or drugs is often a consequence of not being able to deal with the stress of negative and difficult things. Having been pummeled by many emotional storms in my own life, I know how easy it is to indulge in whatever makes you feel better, even for a brief moment. Dreaming of a new pair of shoes or eating half a dozen doughnuts is a wonderful short-term distraction from thinking about a loved one dying or your marriage crumbling.

The key word with the Temperance card is not *abstinence,* but *moderation*. Nor do I recommend my clients go into either bars or shopping malls with hatchets and hack apart the displays. Shopping, overeating, and some of the other behavioral addictions are trickier to deal with than drugs or drink. I say this because no one needs to ever drink alcohol or get high again, but everyone needs to eat something or buy things to live or function in society. Learning moderation can be a harder path than swearing off something altogether. The lesson the Fool learns in this station is that moderation is needed in everything, including moderation.

The Temperance card can also be a warning sign of being too frugal. We all know people who are annoyingly cheap—the ones who, when the waiter brings the check, disappear from the table into the restroom. I had one client whose wealthy in-laws gave her a ball of twine for Christmas each year. One classic interpretation of this card is that the angel is pouring water into wine; maybe that inspired a cheapskate friend of mine to dilute the bottles of Scotch he serves to guests.

Temperance is very much a relationship card, although it may not seem so at first. Unless we choose to live by ourselves like the Unabomber in a shack in the mountains, we have to figure out how to get along with other people. More of a challenge is how to "temper" ourselves in a love relationship or marriage.

I was at a wedding a while back. At one point in the service, the bride and groom each took a tapered candle and, using their separate flames, jointly lit the wick of a single large candle—a popular way of symbolizing the merging of two souls into one. At this particular wedding when the groom moved toward the big candle, he accidentally knocked it over, sending melting wax all over the bride's gown. I don't want to call it an omen, but the marriage lasted only a few years. The couple could not compromise on anything. He wanted to live in New York, she wanted to live in LA; she wanted kids, he didn't; she had a dog, he liked cats; and on and on. Maturity means compromise, and not always getting our way is a gnarly lesson in life.

All good relationships must strike a balance or they die. That balance might seem unbalanced to outsiders, but it may not be. Let me introduce Roxanne and her husband, Mitch. They are no spring chickens; in fact they just celebrated their fiftieth anniversary. For fifty years this is the way they've lived: Mitch gets up before his wife and makes her a lavish breakfast, which he brings to her on a tray in bed. After she eats she goes back to sleep while he cleans the house. Midmorning, when Roxanne has finally gotten herself ready, Mitch asks her what she would like to do, and whatever it is he does it. Mitch is the guy you see sitting outside the store in his car patiently reading the newspaper while his wife goes shopping. He is the guy loaded down like a mule at the airport, balancing five suitcases while his wife totes a little purse. Mitch lives to please his "bride," he is as smitten with her as he was the day they married, and even though no one on the outside gets it, it works for them. They have tempered their relationship in unequal but satisfying proportions. Not everything needs to be fifty–fifty; it just has to feel right to you.

I would like to say a word or two about alchemy, a term that often is used when discussing the Temperance card. And I mean a word or two, because that is my entire depth of knowledge on the subject. It is not because I have not tried. Ten years ago I was at a mystical bookstore in California and bought a huge and authoritative-looking book on this subject. I imagined adding the word *alchemist* to my résumé— how cool would that be! A month after delving into this book headlong, I came to the end and realized I did not understand a single thing I had read beyond: In days of old alchemists tried to turn base metals into gold (and failed). Alchemists tried to find the Elixir of Life that cured all illnesses (and failed). Alchemists searched for the Philosopher's Stone that promised knowledge of everything (and failed). My hope to blithely throw around terms like *nigredo, citrinitas,* and *Sacrae Particulae* was dashed. I had to scrap my plans to invest heavily in chalices and beakers. What was the point of being an alchemist if everything you tried was for naught?

Years later a metaphysically oriented friend of mine disavowed me of my simple notions. Alchemy may not have literally been able to turn lead into gold, but it is still a good symbolic evocation of man's path to enlightenment. Carl Jung noted that the very act of searching for these goals changed the mind and spirit of the alchemist himself. Tangentially, the experiments in alchemy also produced a score of break-throughs and discoveries that the modern world could not do without, including forming the basis of modern chemistry and introducing the studies of metalwork, glass manufactur-ing, distilling, leather tanning, embalming, pharmaceuticals, gunpowder, cosmetics, and a slew of other things. Alchemy was far from a failure; although it never reached its glorious original goal, the fallout from the experiments was profound.

So how does this relate to you when you draw the Tem-perance card? Life is an experiment, and sometimes we set out to do one thing and wind up inventing something else. We mix oil and water, water and fire, oil and vinegar (yum), fire and rocks, and see what we get. It is not immediately apparent what the result might be. It could be brilliant, toxic, or just dull. But like Jung suggested, the act of trying changes us. While the Temperance card is about moderation, it is also paradoxically about experimentation and boldness. Without testing the waters, without putting one foot on the shore and the other in the pond, we can't move ahead.

Being foolish is different from being curious. No inven-tion in the history of the world would have happened if someone had not thought, *I wonder what would happen if I* . . . Temperance is not about being a prude or shutting down your creativity; it is the wise man's path of life. Move ahead judiciously, but move. Experiment safely but experiment.

THE DEVIL

THE DEVIL

CARD NUMBER 15

The devil tempts all men, but idle men tempt the devil.
—ARABIAN PROVERB

Today I am sitting at my desk; it is a warm sunny day. I have the French doors open, and the brightly colored birds are going to town on the new seeds in the feeder. Elmer, my little bulldog, is gently snoring at my feet and I can hear in the distance my neighbor's children laughing as they play on the grass. All in all it is a flawless summer day, a perfectly inappropriate time to talk about Satan, ultimate evil, and being trapped in darkness.

But let's start at the beginning. Do you believe in the devil? Do you believe in evil? I do. Maybe not so much a literal winged fallen angel with a pitchfork and a grudge, but I utterly believe that evil is as much a force in the world and in ourselves as good is. There are as many kinds of evil as there are flavors of gourmet jelly beans. The obvious ones are those that cause harm to the innocent, evident through stealing and lying and generally being a crappy person. If people murder others, it does not take a great stretch of imagination to declare them evil; the same for cheaters, manipulators, sexual predators, or cult leaders with frosty pitchers of Kool-Aid. These people are Evil with a capital *E,* and although you will read about them every day in the newspaper you may not actually ever meet such high-profile creeps in your life. If you were a tarot reader doing a reading for Charles Manson or Hitler and the Devil card flipped over, it would be par for the course. Strangely, even though I do not hang out with monsters of mythic proportion, the Devil card is very active in my readings. In more subtle terms I find that it is a very telling marker of dark addictions of the soul. I do not mean alcoholism or even drug addiction (these show up more often with the Temperance card), but rather the negative addictive process that keeps us doing the same hurtful things over and over. This is far more common than you might imagine.

What does one make of my client Gina, who can't remove herself from a ten-year illicit affair with a married man? People have affairs for a hundred different reasons, some more harmful than others. Gina's affair in particular falls under the rubric of the Devil card because there is absolutely not one positive aspect to it except "great sex" (and even that I suspect is a rationalization on Gina's part to explain away her wildly masochistic behavior). Gina is a well-regarded dancer in a New York City ballet company. As a ballerina she is an expert when it comes to self-control and saying no. She counts calories, does Pilates, goes to the massage therapist, and never misses a rehearsal. I am telling you this because Gina knows how to take care of herself beautifully except for this one aspect of her life—which is destroying her. She is metaphorically chained around the neck to this demon lover.

The married man whom she has been with all these years treats her like a dog. When he wants her he calls, and she runs to him. When she wants something from him, he is not available. He and his relatives steal money from her. He has a dozen other girlfriends whom he makes sure she knows about. He sleeps with whores and compares them to her. He sends her cell phone pictures of his other girlfriends' naked bodies. In ten years he has never bought her a gift or a meal. If they travel together, he leaves her in motel rooms when he goes off with his friends for dinner or a show at a strip club. He is selfish and sleazy and rude, but she cannot tear herself away from him. All the rational discussion and salient talking points I or her friends engage in are met with profound head nods and promises, but none of us believes for a second that she will not run back to him at his first phone call. This woman's lover is for her the devil. He takes her soul apart one piece at a time, robs her of respect and self-esteem, and leaves an empty shell where there once was a person.

There comes a point in dealing with the Ginas of the world where all advice fails. Gina is not my only client like this; there are many others like her with whom progress is not possible. They are so enthralled with something bad that it is as if they are truly bedeviled and under a spell. At times like this I wish I were an exorcist instead of a tarot reader, because I feel I am up against an adversary far bigger than me. Most serious addictions are powered in this otherworldly way. What gives a drug, a drink, or a human being such big hoodoo that an otherwise rational person, who knows better, has no say in the matter? The drug-drink-man spell holds the reins and calls the shots. I find *the devil* is as good a term to use as any more modern therapy-driven labels for this behavior.

A few religions of the world speak of predestination, believing that you walk a path that is set out for you from birth to death, and free will does not enter into it. This is certainly one way of throwing up your hands, dealing with bad behavior as some sort of karmic package that you are working out in this lifetime. This is a bit too sad for my taste, and so I go to the cards to find—if not answers—then understanding. The Fool, whose journey we are watching, meets the devil in the second half of his journey. The Fool may be finding it increasingly difficult to drag himself away from his baser instincts and, just as happens in real life when we are feeling weak, something or somebody shows up to tempt him. I think almost all of us at some point, when torn between long-term goals versus a short-term fix, choose the latter. Being "good" often feels just too difficult. But the problem is that the more we slip, the harder it becomes to get back on the right path. The devil is a great seducer, and the Fool, being a mere mortal, falls for the trickster's promises of fun and frolic. It is not for nothing that in the Rider-Waite deck the Devil card looks like the Lovers card in reverse. The Lovers card depicts a man and a woman in a flowering garden beneath the sheltering wings of an angel. In the Devil card, two people stand facing each other chained around the neck; hovering over them is a goat-footed horned devil. Even more dramatic is the rendering of the devil in the Bohemian Gothic Tarot deck. It is both hotly sexy and awful. A leathery winged demon holds a pale swooning woman in his arms as he jabs her with a lethal syringe. This image perfectly captures the seductive power of evil.

I have to admit that even though I am culturally Jewish, I have a predilection for watching hellfire-and-brimstone preachers on TV. These pastel-suited gentlemen with the windswept coiffures and shiny white shoes speak about the devil not as an abstract concept, but as familiar as an unsavory next-door neighbor, as visceral as anyone in their viewing audience. I love it when the preacher becomes swept away with the Holy Ghost, speaking in tongues and like an advancing army smiting the devil by placing his hand on the sinner's head. These evangelists deal with the devil the way I deal with a raccoon that gets into my trash barrels: nothing subtle, just make lots of noise and drive it away.

Over the years I have found that those who overcome their addictions have some sort of faith base. Some go to church, others believe in a higher power, some just have a sense of being part of a bigger plan. Calling on that energy for release from pain appears to be a great source of power. The Ginas I know believe in nothing beyond their own small pleasures and daily existence. There is nothing for them before life or after life, so really, what does it all matter? They live in a cold lonely void and grab pleasure where they can, even if pleasure is actually pain in disguise, because feeling something is better than feeling nothing.

I think at some point in our lives we each ask ourselves the big question, *What does it all mean?* "Nothing" is one answer, and this bleak viewpoint has given the world some profound poetry, fiction, and art. Those who think this way are not particularly happy; they may have proven to themselves that life is a passing illusion or a cosmic joke, but does it give the Fool or us any traction on the difficult path toward the light? For me the answer is no.

How does the devil seduce us? Let me count the ways. First is what we have just been talking about: feeling hollow and believing that you have no real purpose on the earth. Second, we're seduced by wasting time; the old adage "Idle hands are the devil's playground" is true. Please don't mistake me for an industrious Amish person; I can be as lazy as the next guy or girl. It's not about sneaking a nap on the couch, but rather having no purpose in life. Everyone needs something to accomplish, be it creating a rocketship or caulking your tub. If you are doing something productive (as opposed to something passive, such as watching TV), you will not be thinking of your addiction, whatever that may be. It is impossible (and believe me I have tried) to think of two things at the same time. Being productive is salt thrown in the devil's eyes.

What else attracts the devil except hopelessness and sloth? Try an open invitation! More people invite the devil into their lives than you may think. Be very careful about keeping the door to the dark realm shut, or you may get more than you bargained for. When I see teenagers playing around with witchcraft or fooling around with satanism as a Goth fashion statement, I get troubled. I have seen people try voodoo curses on their exes and black magic spells on enemies. Dipping into the dark side might seem like a last resort or a way to bring control into your life, or even a fun thing to dabble in, but it often has the opposite effect.

———•———

There are also some objects that I would caution you to avoid. I shy very far away from Ouija boards. I have seen them open doors between worlds that are best left shut. One of the problems with Ouija boards is they are sold as a harmless game, but the innocent souls who fish off this deep end may be surprised by what they hook.

There are other objects I try to keep out of my life. It is both a random and rather silly-sounding list, but for me opals, English ivy, and peacock feathers—to name a few— have a very long and well-proven negative cause-and-effect outcome. Opal happens to be my birthstone, ivy is pretty, and peacock feathers are nice too (although I prefer them on a living peacock rather than in a vase), but every time these things have entered my life (or that of my clients), bad things have happened. On the other hand black cats, the number thirteen, and that sort of stuff seems to me not a problem. Again, this is all personal; various objects may affect you one way, while others not at all. If you feel an aversion to something, avoid it. You may not be able to put a finger on why you feel this way, but listen to your inner voice.

Another negative thing to have around is a partial deck of tarot cards. Tarot cards like to stay together like the family they are. Never throw out a used or incomplete deck; instead wrap them in silk and bury them in the backyard or a park as a sign of respect. Similarly, be careful of icons and items that you put in your house. Voodoo dolls and implements, satanic symbols, and pictures of death and destruction are unhealthy to live with and, as my mother would say when I wore my sweater too tight, "attract the wrong kind of attention."

Let's say you have an opal ring, a collection of Nazi memorabilia, a voodoo doll, an ivy-covered cottage, and a bunch of peacock feathers. What do you do with them? This is a difficult question. The easiest is the ivy (pull it out and get rid of it); same with things of no value like the feathers. But what about the other items, especially an opal ring? You will not like my answer, but I will tell you just what I tell my clients: Get rid of them. Now here is the rub. When I say get rid of something, I do not mean give it to a friend or profit by selling it on eBay or the like. You will not get any brownie points by passing along an accursed item to someone else. Just divest yourself of it. Leave it on a park bench, throw it in the pond, toss it in the air and walk away. You may be surprised at how light and unencumbered you feel afterward.

By now I can see you looking up from this book and shaking your head. You previously trusted me, and now I am telling you to throw your grandmother's jewelry in the air and run away. It sounds a bit nutty, I admit, but if you are really at your wit's end and just do not know why a bad situation will not resolve itself . . . well, I will leave the rest to you.

Let me make one thing quite clear here. I do not think these items are "cursed"; they just attract bad energy. If someone says you are cursed, you are probably with someone who wants to fleece you. One reason tarot card readers have a bad name is that the kind found in dilapidated storefronts with a neon sign routinely run scams that go like this: The worried client walks in and sits down at a table. The reader puts some cards on the table, and a look of horror crosses her face. She informs the client that he is cursed, but (thank goodness she came in time) she can reverse this. How much will it cost? It depends on if he is wearing a Rolex or a Timex, if his clothing is from T. J. Maxx or Neiman Marcus. If the client looks wealthy, the curse will cost a lot to lift and will require many sessions.

To prove there is a curse, the fortune-teller goes behind the curtain and returns with an egg. She cracks the egg in a bowl and blood runs out. The client gasps, and the reader has sealed the deal. When the client's wallet is drained, a fresh egg is broken and is now clear of blood; the curse has been lifted. The "blood" in the egg is usually red ink or chicken blood injected into the egg with a very fine-gauge needle. It is a scam, but a powerful one, used on people in crisis. These storefront fortune-tellers have many tricks like this, so be careful about whom you let peer into your soul.

THE TOWER

THE TOWER

A Broken Fortune is like a falling column; the lower it sinks the greater weight it has to sustain.

—Ovid

If you are buying real estate, may I suggest it not be in or near a tower. Towers, which loom large in history as well as the present day, are less the Ayn Rand symbols of man's heroic nature and more the architectural version of sticking a Kick Me sign on some poor sap's back. Towers, with their prideful escape from gravity, just invite those who want to knock them down.

The Tower card has always been ominous. In sequence it follows the Devil card, and there is no deck to my knowledge that depicts the Tower in any way but scary. In most decks the Tower is being struck by lightning, it is on fire, and people are in free fall from its windows. It is a scene of utter chaos and destruction. In some decks the Tower is an actual tower, in others a tree that has been struck by lightning. One of the alternate names for this card is Lightning, and strangely one of the earliest known important tarot decks, the Visconti-Sforza, does not contain this card at all. Was it an oversight? Was it just too terrible to depict?

The meaning of this card is clear. It speaks of crisis, chaos, and downfall. Awfulness will befall you, and not in a subtle way, but rather as an explosive depth charge of misery. Even dealt reversed the Tower card is a sorry sight. Upside down it still means awful things are afoot, but you might have a slight chance to escape with your life.

For those tarot readers and students who a decade ago got cocky with the metaphorical nature of the cards, September 11, 2001, brought us all back to reality. I showed this Major Arcana card in a lecture I gave once, and then followed with a slide of real people falling from the blazing Twin Towers. The reaction was visceral; at the end of the talk, a few people approached me and said I should not have shown that image. It was too disturbing, to show it seemed almost obscene.

Now, I must step in here and remind my readers that the Tower card does not always mean literal architectural destruction. Many tarot scholars *do* continue to use it metaphorically, and link it to the best-laid plans getting derailed or someone's out-of-control ego. The tarot card of a tower under attack translates to someone too big for his britches, with a huge ego, who is about to get his comeuppance.

If this card does not directly refer to you or someone you love, it can be lots of fun to see greedy awful people brought to their knees—the very things they cling to destroyed. When devious big shots lose their mansions in the Hamptons, lose their club memberships, and see their Ferraris repoed, it gives us a charge. It is a big ol' schadenfreude hoedown.

But imagine that in your reading you repeatedly draw the Tower; then this card refers to you. Maybe you don't have a mansion or a sports car, but as the Bible says, you are "prideful." You do think you are better than others, you reside in an "ivory tower," and you do look down your nose from your great height at the less fortunate or polished. Although you may pretend to be aw-shucks modest, you are most assuredly full of yourself, and behind your back few people have a nice word to say about you. As the saying goes, "Pride goeth before a fall," and there's no bigger fall in the works than the kind indicated by drawing the Tower card. If you are lucky, drawing this card will be a wake-up call to change your snarky, self-serving ways. If you are not so lucky (or do not heed advice well, which often goes with being a big narcissistic know-it-all), you might want to go to bed, pull the covers up over your head, and stay there for the next decade. Remember, the bigger they are the harder they fall, and no one (including fate) gets excited knocking over an anthill.

Is there any upside to the Tower card? Sure, there is an upside to everything, but it will not make the imminent destruction go away. The Tower card is not a get-out-of-jail-free card. You will be called upon to walk through the fire and lose your pride, or be consumed by the flames. After all, life as you know it is about to be wiped away, and once the bottom has been hit, then what happens? You assess your losses, make new decisions, get a fresh start, and rebuild—or you curl up and die. Some tarot scholars believe that it is not until the Tower card has swept away all the dysfunction and pride that man can enter a pure state of consciousness. It is the calm after the storm. Once the dust has cleared, you are open to a new vision, one not clouded by power, money, and wrong beliefs.

Let us not forget that the Tower card comes *after* the Devil card. What is that all about? Let's ask the Fool, on whose journey the cards are built. By this time the fool is no longer the naive child; he has been roughed up a bit, challenged and guided by teachers, exposed to new ideas. He has also been swayed by the devil. The devil is a great seducer, and why should the Fool be any less taken with the glitz and glam of the good life than we mortals? The devil has whispered in the Fool's ear that he is Joe Cool, hot stuff, very important. The cool Fool struts about filled with big plans; yes, he would be quite at home living in a tower where he could look down at the "little people." A tower seems safe, impenetrable, and majestic—sort of like one of Donald Trump's buildings. Of course this is an illusion because the Tower is built with the faulty bricks of man's ego and is ripe for destruction. For a brief while the Fool is in love with the Tower, but then it happens: The fog clears and he sees the tower as the abomination it is—and at that very moment lightning strikes and the seemingly impervious thing crumbles to the ground. The ease with which it falls proves that it was a construct of the mind and not a real thing, although as we have learned real brick-and-mortar towers collapse too. It was a hologram of lies and conceits. This towering inferno (just like in the movie of that name) is nothing more than special effects; it is not real and it never was.

And so again, the Fool finds himself at a crossroads; can he move forward and rebuild something more meaningful than the Tower? Should he just throw up his hands in dismay and give up? The concept of "moving on" is easy to say and hard to do. I have seen many ways that people cope with this situation. Some of my clients shut the past in a mental box and refuse to think about or examine it. Others get stuck in an endless cycle of "why, why, why"; they go from friends, to shrinks, to clergy, to self-help books hoping to find an answer. A few lucky ones are motivated enough by the crisis to get their lives in better order. They see that life is not forever, and that worshiping the material is not in the end worthwhile. They come to grips with the fact that everything changes, people leave or die, jobs end, children grow up and move away. Happiness is not a permanent state of being, change is.

Carl Jung, who incorporated the symbolism of the tarot deck into his theories, was intrigued by the theme of chaos. Remember, the Tower card speaks of things falling apart, of being in free fall without a safety net. Because Jung believed that mankind shares a collective unconscious, he found it not surprising that dreams of falling are not limited to one culture or age. The common interpretation of this sort of dream is as an indication of anxiety or deep-rooted insecurity. Falling feels like being out of control; as awful as the fall is, hitting the ground may be even worse. Most dreamers wake up before they hit the ground, with a startling body movement known by the scientific name of a myclonic jerk. Its seismic force is often felt by our bedmate.

In the Bible and in classical psychiatry both, dreams of falling are uncomfortable omens. Biblically, falling is a result of not being in line with the Lord's teaching, literally a fall from grace. Freud (being Freud) gave the falling dream a sexual connotation. To Freud, it represented the fear of giving in to a sexual urge. Interestingly enough, towers falling with lightning and flames appear to share the exact same symbolism from culture to culture. From the Tower of Babel to the Twin Towers, a collapsing tower always bespeaks disaster. If something that important can be struck down, how can any of us feel safe?

———•———

One more story: I was sent to High Point, North Carolina, by the *New York Times* to write an article on shopping for furniture there. I hooked up with a group of seven women from Grosse Point, Michigan, wealthy ladies who came every few years to refurnish their entire houses. These were serious shoppers, and if I had any doubt it was banished as I watched as one of the ladies accidentally walked out of an open loading door on the third floor of the building. Because new furniture was being lifted to that level by a crane, she thought that the open door led to another showroom, and so eager to see more couches and tables was she that she stepped out into nothingness.

She fell three flights, landing facedown in the concrete parking strip. What followed next is something I will never forget. As we all screamed 911, she suddenly began to move, slowly, shaking one body part after another. Then she stood up, dusted off her bouclé Chanel suit, and walked back into the ground floor of the showroom to continue shopping. I have never seen anything like this except in superhero cartoons. That night I asked her if she was all right. She was on the tour with her sister, who was a nurse. They both assured me she was fine. "But how could you be?" I asked. "I had a task to complete and I just could not give up," she replied.

The Fool in the tarot deck falls off a cliff, and a lady from Grosse Point falls out the door of a furniture showroom. They both live to see another day. The point of life is that we all have a task to complete (even if at times we forget what it is, or it involves something as mundane as buying a sofa) and if we stop moving forward, we die. The devil tempts us, our egos crash and burn, our best-laid plans fall down at our feet, but if we decide to call it a day and live among the wreckage, we are calling it quits. Many tarot readers feel that the Tower is the worst card in the deck. If the Death card makes clients want to run out the door, the Tower makes the reader want to leave.

How do you sit calmly at the table when a tarot reader tells you your world is about to blow apart? This card can be a tough hurdle to overcome, but keep in mind that no matter what the dire situation is at present, every card in the deck is about progress toward a happy end.

The Tower card pops up in popular culture. In J. K. Rowling's wonderfully imaginative novel *Harry Potter and the*

Half Blood Prince, chapter 27 is called "The Lightning-Struck Tower." It refers to the Astronomy Tower at Hogwarts, the tallest and most ominous building of all. The battle there is foretold by Professor Trelawney with her tarot cards: "Calamity, Disaster, coming nearer all the time," she incants.

One of the reasons I do not like, and seldom do, one-card readings is that they are dead ends. The cards in the deck relate to other cards; they are amplified by or diminished by what is around them. No card (no matter how powerful) stands alone. To draw the Tower card and no others is too depressing and scary. Okay, so your life as you know it will explode, fall apart, and disappear. What has caused this, and what will happen after the crisis is over? That is why we need other cards in a reading. Even I (an alarmist when I am feeling relaxed, a veritable Cassandra when I am cranky) can't work with one card. And so I don't.

Allow me once more to present a medical model. Using the Tower card as a single draw is like a physician coming into the examining room and saying you have a dreadful disease based solely on one symptom. For a true diagnosis a doctor, like a tarot card reader, needs much more information.

So the best way to deal with this tarot card is to break it down into manageable parts. If the Tower is followed by the Star card or some other hopeful omen, this should let you know all is well. If medical matters, financial matters, or relationship issues are what the Tower relates to, then you can make changes in that aspect of your life. If your tarot reader just starts swaying in her chair like Professor Trelawney with a look of terror on her face, ask her to push the reading forward and give you answers. Doom and gloom in your future is not enough to go on.

Some readers get a kick out of scaring their clients; they like to have clients think that the course of events is in their control. No tarot reader has that power. If we did we would rule the world, or at least win PowerBall every few weeks. This is one reason why I stay away from witchcraft. All the potions and spells may make you feel like you are accomplishing something, but in fact you are not doing anything. A reader reads the future; only God (in whatever form you see him, her, or it) can decide our fate. Of course I offer suggestions; if I see a heart attack in the cards, I will tell my client to see a doctor. If I see financial loss, I will discuss that. But again, neither I nor any other reader can change your life without your dedicated effort and a bit of good luck.

Not all falling apart is the same. Losing a job is not like losing your spouse, which is also not like losing your health. They are all crises, to be sure, but how they are dealt with and the long-term outcome can be very selective. Whether your accountant is stealing from you, or your husband is cheating on you, or the herbal porridge your health guru recommends makes you nauseous, you need to identify the crisis before you can take the proper steps. Don't be overwhelmed by the Tower card; it is just another stumbling block on your road to a better life, and once you have relieved yourself of your impediments you will feel brighter and happier.

THE STAR

THE STAR

CARD NUMBER 17

Happiness isn't a goal, it's a by-product.

—ELEANOR ROOSEVELT

Some would say that the Star card is the hippie flower child of the tarot deck, all about love and peace and all that. The Star card is astrologically linked to the sign of the water bearer Aquarius, and the Age of Aquarius is not mired in the hot mess of some more dark or combative signs like Aries and Scorpio, but instead brings hope for the future and visions of all being well.

The Star card is the cookie and glass of milk offered to us after the Tower card has exploded and thrown our life into chaos. It is a deep exhalation, a sense that things will come together and make sense.

As a reader it took me a long time to appreciate this card. Many a time I treated the Star card like a sappy and sentimental Hallmark card, a sort of tarot version of "and they lived happily ever after." It seemed thin in character to me, needlessly optimistic, and not as profound as some of the other rock 'em sock 'em Major Arcana cards. But then I lived life, and as I got older and wiser I came to realize that the Star card is what keeps the human race putting one foot ahead of another and moving forward instead of giving up.

I would, however, like to rename this card from the Star to hope, the best emotional currency in the world because it leaves the door open so a ray of light can illuminate the darkness. This truly is what this card is all about.

You have to have lived life fully to understand the need for and the power of hope. It is what many of us cling to in order to get through the day. When we or someone we love gets ill, when we lose a loved one, when our marriage falls apart, when our bank account disappears, hope is what's left for us to cling to. Even million-to-one odds sound better than no hope at all. Just as they say there are no atheists in foxholes, there are no clients of mine in terrible situations who do not breathe a great sigh of relief when the Star card hits the table.

I have heard people refer to the Star as the light-at-the-end-of-the-tunnel card. When I used this phrase with one client, he asked how I knew if it really was the light at the end of the tunnel, versus a train coming to mow him down. The Star card asks us to believe that it is the former, not the latter. We must go on faith that the universe wants the best for us and is not out to get us.

Sally, a favorite client, has been wrestling with this card for years. If you ask her whether she's an optimist or a pessimist, she'll say she is a very optimistic person, someone to whom the metaphorical glass is always half full. But this is not the case. She is caught in a complete cycle of despair and sees no hope at all. She asks me questions about her problems and then answers them herself. And whatever she is talking about—her troubling health, her lack of a love life, her losing her job—is in her view immutable; there is no hope or solution. When I talk to her about options, I see her shutting down and blanking out.

There is a story I tell my clients that I will share with you. I am sure this is not exactly as I heard it, but you can still get the point. A man is standing on his roof as floodwaters rise around him. He is terrified, lifts his hands to God, and implores, "Lord save me, for I will drown." The water continues to rise around him and in the distance he sees a horse paddling his way in the flood. He watches as it swims by. Again he raises his hands heavenward. "Lord help me, I am sure to drown." This time a large log floats by as he watches. Finally as he asks the Lord one more time to save him, he sees a rickety rowboat with no oars drift by. While he watches it move out of sight, the floodwaters rise and he drowns. Suddenly both wet and furious, he finds himself face-to-face with Saint Peter at heaven's gate. "Didn't you hear me?" he says. "I called out three times for God to save my life! Now let me in and get me some dry clothes!" Saint Peter looks sadly at him and, as he is closing the gate keeping this poor soul out, shrugs and says, "Yes, we heard you . . .

who do you think sent the horse, the log, and the boat? You did nothing to help yourself with the tools we gave you."

The point of this story is that salvation often looks quite different than we picture it. The man on the roof was expecting a sleek Coast Guard vessel or a high-tech helicopter rescue lift. Because his salvation was less than picture-perfect, he ignored help and drowned.

Back to Sally and her hopeless situation. She is a fatal perfectionist: No job offered perfectly matches her talents, no man without movie-star looks need call her for a date, she still lives with her parents at age forty-five because she can't find a nice enough house on her salary. No doctor can help her medical woes, no shrink can fix her emotional issues, and you might as well throw me into the mix as another lousy person who has yet to help her out. Her life is a litany of letdowns and it is all so sad.

The funny thing is that she often draws the Star card in readings. I do think that the same Almighty who sent the horse, the log, and the rowboat to the drowning man is watching out for Sally, but like the man on the roof she would sooner drown than compromise on halfway measures and save herself.

The point I am trying to make is that getting the Star card is a wonderful and auspicious sign, but it still means *you* have to do the legwork and make your own good fortune.

Beyond acting on faith in the future, or a sign of the end of a torturous phase of life, the Star card gives suggestions on how to reach this epiphany. Sally thinks of no one but herself; to her, the rest of the world is populated with vaguely sketched cartoon characters, not real people with needs and wants. To be a complete person and find salvation demands that you open your heart and soul to others. As a volunteer EMT I hear over and over again from my fellow emergency workers that the times they are at their finest are when they are helping another person. It is a high that no drug or alcohol can match. To save a life, to hold a hand, to offer a shoulder for someone else to cry on is the biggest gift you can give yourself.

———•———

Let's pick up again on the long, complicated path of the Fool. He has just witnessed the destruction of the Tower. His ego, his wealth, his position in society have all been lost. He is back to square one. It is now his decision to pick up and move on or give up. In following the Tower card, the Star card tells him he can move forward and find happiness. The Star is an indication that all will again be well. He has lost everything, but he still has his life, which is the greatest blessing. The Star's light is probably the same inexplicable light that we still see shining in the faces of those in unbearable predicaments.

Now let me tell you about another client, Roberta, a huge fan of self-visualization. This trend has been around for a very long time. Starting decades back with Napoleon Hill's *Think and Grow Rich,* and continuing to more current titles like *The Secret, How to Get Rich, Think Like a Billionaire,* and *The Magic of Thinking Big,* books and speakers have stressed that if we can conceive of something, we can attain it. I have a number of friends who swear that this method works for them. They visualize a house by the seashore, and five years later they are living in a house by the seashore. They dream of owning a BMW, and a BMW enters their life. Obviously, some people are better at this than others. Personally I have never been able to visualize into reality a cold can of Coke on a hot day. It comes back to the Star card and the story about the man on the roof.

One thing for sure is that sitting in a chair visualizing things is not enough. If it were, we would have to duck as big-screen televisions, Porsches, Louis Vuitton handbags, and laptops came flying through the air en route to their visualizing owners. Knowing what you want in life is terrific, though, and why not have a very real image in your mind of what it looks like? What color hydrangeas will you plant around your seaside cottage? What type of leather do you want in the Beemer? Roberta may think that imagining these things makes them magically happen, when in fact what makes them happen is that she is goal-oriented and a hard worker. I am sure that no matter what Roberta sets her mind on she will get, because she is relentless until she accomplishes her task at hand. There is little magic when focused people achieve their goals, which is the way life works. Show me the lazy couch potato who has all the fancy stuff and a trophy wife, and I will show you someone who bought the lucky lottery ticket at the 7-Eleven.

The old saying "Genius is 1 percent inspiration and 99 percent perspiration" is apt. No one looks at a brain surgeon and groans, "Oh you are so lucky, that's the job I want." I can assure you that every restaurant critic, rock star, theatrical makeup artist, movie director, talk-show host, and book author hears this on a regular basis. People do not understand or appreciate the hard work and talent that go into other people's jobs. A lady in the town I reside in once said to me, "My ten-year-old son loves to eat; he should have your job at *Gourmet*." I smiled at her and walked on.

I do not throw the term *karma* around loosely because it makes me feel that I should be wearing a rainbow headband and a peace-sign T-shirt. But the Star card can't be clearly explained without dipping into that term. Karma, as you may know, can be summed up as "what goes around comes around." You do something dastardly to someone and think you have gotten away with it, but the universe has some rather unsavory plans for you yet. Similarly, a good deed does not go unnoticed by the forces that shape our lives. Karma is good to know about for revenge seekers because if you believe in the law of karma, you need not do the dirty work yourself. In the fullness of time "they" will get theirs.

In addition to the major aspects of the Star card—hope, generosity, having faith, and being serene—it has one more aspect: becoming motivated and being creatively inspired. The Star card can represent the big "aha" moment when the cartoon lightbulb over Einstein's head begins to glow. Short of an orgasm, there are few moments in our lives more satisfying than when things fall into place and we "get it." We may have a spark of creativity on the grand scale of Mozart or Dostoyevsky, or maybe we finally understand long division. There are many levels of an "aha" moment, and each one has the seal of the Star card on it.

THE MOON

THE MOON

CARD NUMBER 18

I became insane, with long intervals of horrible sanity.
—EDGAR ALLAN POE

As a reader, I find the Moon card wildly appealing. My dark side gets all hot and bothered by what it represents: occult forces, danger, craziness, and more. It is spooky and ominous and utterly delicious.

Many years ago the moon represented insanity, or lunacy, derived from the word *luna,* "moon." Lunatics were alleged to become worse during the full moon, when werewolves got into action as well, zombies left their tombs, and dogs howled. Blue moons, moons red with blood, hunter's moons, and eclipses are all fraught with symbolism. To this day it is standard folklore that police stations and emergency rooms are very busy when the moon is full.

The Moon card relates to the old saying in tarot (attributed to Hermes Trismegistus, a mythic representation of a blending of the Greek god Hermes and the Egyptian god Thoth), "That which is above is the same as that which is below." Shortened the saying reads, "As above, so below." *Below what?* one wonders. *And is it true?*

The saying (which is also popular in witchcraft and alchemy, neither of which I dabble in) has to do with the interconnectedness of everything in the universe. We are all conglomerations of atoms and spinning molecules, and in theory there is no real difference between a man, a chair, a planet, or a handbag on sale at Marshalls. I agree in theory with this, but in my tarot readings I find the "one for all, all for one" business not in the least bit helpful. My clients come to me for answers to contemporary problems, not lectures in molecular physics.

The way I prefer to use the Moon card in my readings is as it relates to the line between the conscious and subconscious mind, and these are decidedly not the same thing. The way we act and what we think in the light of the day when fully awake are often the opposite of our subconscious thoughts and dream states. Life below can be as murky and hard to grasp as a catfish swimming at the bottom of a muddy pond, which makes even more sense because the Moon card also represents Cancer, an astrological water sign.

Most of us are somewhat disconnected from "what lies below" in our own lives. This is called denial and can be very useful. I know people who never remember their dreams and claim to be up and down, inside and out exactly what you see on the surface. When I hear this I smile politely but I do not buy it, because none of us is that deeply perky and sweet within.

The Moon card encompasses fears and phobias, night terrors, narcissism, and being stymied by indecision. It is like looking through a glass darkly and seeing a distorted image of things. The Rider-Waite deck's version of this card shows a crescent moon with a human profile within the circle of the full moon. The moon has rays coming off it like the sun. Between two pillars are a dog and a wolf, both baying at the moon, and from the river flowing along the card's foreground a creature is emerging onto land. Many tarot books call this thing a crawfish, as if this were a Cajun seafood boil and not a tarot card; I say it is a scorpion, because the astrological sign Scorpio is both a water sign and a symbol of what lies below. Whatever the shelled creature is, its climbing out of the water is symbolic of our base animalistic nature trying to take hold, or the difficult and sometimes deathly seeming prospect of exploring our own subconscious. Do not forget that the scorpion is a poisonous and scary thing (unlike the dopey edible crawfish).

Few of my clients like the Moon card when I start digging into their emotional underpinnings. They want answers, and when they draw the Moon they get questions that, unless I remember to harness my formidable Scorpio powers of interrogation, might feel intrusive. Traditionally the Moon card dealt right-side up speaks of hidden dangers, enemies pretending to be friends, curses, fears. Could it be any worse reversed? It is one of the few tarot cards where the reverse is actually better. Dealt reversed the moon card still refers to awful creepy things but not quite as dramatically as right-side up—it softens the danger.

Over the years I have noticed that a particular group of my clients always draw this card. They are not "lunatics" by a long shot, but in twenty-first-century parlance they do suffer from depression and anxiety, and often are not dealing correctly with this condition.

Allow me to share a rather personal story with you. I became a convert to the power of medication when I myself was sucked into the morass of depression. Coming from a family of well-known and highly respected but old-school psychiatrists and psychoanalysts, I was of the firm belief that any problem could be talked away. When my uncles were in practice, psychotropic drugs were crude and often ineffective. They were the chemical version of a lobotomy. If talking was good enough for Freud, it was good enough for my uncles and for me. Later, when over a course of five years a clinical depression immobilized me like a spider's web, I talked and talked and talked to my shrink and got worse by the week.

As it turned out it was my general physician who waved the red flag on how badly depressed I was. He had not seen me in a while and when I showed up in his office complaining of pains all over my body (a symptom of depression) and was literally unable to finish my sentences, he wrote me a script for Prozac. Like a good Freudian acolyte holding up the honor of my family, I put the Prozac in a drawer and did not take it. After two months of sinking even farther down, unable to get off the couch, not wanting to get dressed or bathe, I finally swallowed a pill. Actually this is not entirely accurate. My husband, distraught over my unraveling, practically pushed the pill down my throat the way we did with our enormous ailing bullmastiffs.

Long story short is that the Prozac worked like a miracle. Within a very short time I was bounding around town, having lunch with friends, and writing up a storm. I had no side effects at all except for the joy of remembering what life was supposed to feel like. Prozac might not work as quickly or as well for everyone, but it was a lifesaver for me.

The reason I am baring these intimate details in this chapter is because it hurts me to the core when I see clients so obviously "white-knuckling" it. They are struggling hard to get through the day and are told by well-meaning friends or relatives to suck it up and try harder. Well, if they could they would, but they can't so they don't.

I believe that the three tarot cards depicting a moon represent different degrees of anxiety and depression: small, medium, and large. The Moon card is the biggie, and when I see it my first thought is that my client may be doing her damnedest to appear bright and sunny when she feels like jumping out the nearest window.

Sometimes I choose to actively intervene, which is not a mandate for the reader of this book to follow suit, but it works for me as a gesture of compassion. Many years ago I had a client I deeply cared about, and although she had been given a script for an antidepressant by her psychiatrist she refused to take it, preferring instead to have her cards read for the answer to why she felt so blue.

Occasionally I will make house calls, something doctors used to do and I wish they still did because how a patient presents herself in public does not always reflect what is really going on. Sometimes seeing someone's home—neat or messy, attractive or depressing, clean or filthy—is a much more accurate indicator of their problems than what they say.

Anyway, I went to this client's home to do a reading. Previously when I had seen her she looked pulled together. But once she ushered me through her front door it was a different story. Trash and clothing littered the floor, dishes were piled in the sink, and her cat's litter box was overflowing. She was too depressed to even make excuses for the mess. So we sat at her kitchen table (piled high with rotten food and unopened mail) and I began to read her cards. Surprise surprise . . . the Moon card dead center. We talked about her depression, which to my amazement she admitted to without any defensiveness. Then she walked into her bedroom, returning with a vial of pills from the drugstore. She plunked them down on the dirty table. "I don't want to take them because I don't want to get addicted to them," she said.

I looked around at the mess her life had become and asked her if she would rather be addicted to paralyzing depression? On and on we went for the hour. When our reading was over, she assumed I would leave. To her dismay I made myself at home on her cluttered couch. "I am not going anywhere until you take a pill," I said bluntly. We had quite a standoff. I sat and read out-of-date magazines and sale flyers while she stomped around the house telling me she needed to be alone.

When before she'd been happy at my presence, she now wanted to get me out of her house so she could lie down, cry, and continue her sick behavior. I looked at my watch as the hours passed, saying again and again, "I will leave when you take your pill" . . . nothing. She pretended to read a book, I sat there. She attempted to do the dishes, I sat there. The one thing she did not do was leave or flush the pills down the toilet, which made me think she did want my help.

The story has a happy ending. She took a pill in my presence, took one the next day, and the next. Her depression lifted, and when I went to her house two months later it was neat and tidy and there was a vase of daffodils on the table. The pills worked for her, and the depression was gone.

Sometimes life makes us exhausted; we want to stop the world and get off. Life can feel like one damn thing after another; no sooner do we pay one bill than another one arrives in the mailbox. At best we get a short respite from these times of stress, but it is never really over until we are worm food. Because the Fool is Everyman on his journey through life, his triumphs and tragedies follow close on each other's heels. The Fool is faced with the ominous psychological baggage of the Moon card right after he has received the blessings of the Star card. Wouldn't he, like the rest of us, simply want to be happy and dispense with the painful psychological probing? You'd think it would be the other way around—first the pain, then the relief—but it isn't. Sometimes I feel great empathy for the Fool; I want to say, "Oh no, not again! I mean you just had the Star!" There are yet more obstacles and pitfalls before him, and his struggle only ended momentarily. But isn't that the case with all of us, and maybe in the end for the best? Think how boring a movie would be with no plot twists or suspense. Think how boring life would be if we were born and we died and nothing happened in the middle.

If we accept the premise that life is hard, we must also respect that it is harder for some of us than for others. What kind of hardships am I referring to? A short list would include childhood sexual molestations, keeping a brutal and dysfunctional marriage together for fear of being alone, being the victim of a violent crime, enduring a serious accident that has altered your way of life forever, or reliving horrible things that you have witnessed during a war. Many of us live our lives through a clever construct of denial and amnesia, and not every person is well served by looking at what lies below through too clear a glass. Only if the client is strong enough to handle these revelations should they be brought up; otherwise leave them be. Without repression and denial many wounded souls would not be able to make it through the day. We edit out what we can't deal with, and that filter should be respected.

Here is an example of the strangely unpleasant side of digging too deeply. I had a client named Kathy who, when we first met, was happy and relatively carefree. She had a few issues to work on but basically life was good. I did not see her again for a year, at which time she resurfaced, looking like she had been through a bombing. Her eyes were haunted, and she seemed like a raw nerve end.

During this interim she had joined up with a hard-line therapy group whose notion of a cure consisted of viciously stripping away each group member's defenses. In the course of a year, happy Kathy had been confronted with the "fact" that she was lazy, fat, stupid, and boring. She had recast her quirky but loving parents into dysfunctional monsters, her hardworking husband into an uncaring workaholic, and her rambunctious but adorable children as suffering from ADHD with oppositional disorder. Her comfy home had become "a bourgeois trap," her scrapbook hobby a "ridiculous waste of time." Instead of a tweak she had been put through the meat grinder. I never saw her again and often wonder what became of her.

There is a vast difference between living a life of self-delusion and being attacked with pointless negativity. I have had people in my life who felt it was their birthright to comment meanly on my weight, hairdo, or choice of outfit whenever they saw me. Another made sure I knew if there was a bad review of my book in the newspaper. A wife of a friend of mine always greeted me with "You look so tired" when she saw me. These verbal slings and arrows hit the target in my tender subconscious where they would hurt the most and the wound would be slowest to heal.

How do you know if someone is really trying to help you or is just getting off on being mean? How do you know if you are truly helping a client and not being an emotional bully? There are no hard-and-fast rules, but I think if it feels more painful than you can stand or your client is cringing when you "speak the truth," that is a good place to stop. People will usually come to insights on their own with just a gentle nudge, and if they resist wildly maybe they know what is best for them. What lies below, for them, might just be better off sitting on the murky bottom.

THE SUN

THE SUN

Card Number 19

If I had to choose a religion, the sun as the universal giver of life would be my god.

—Napoleon Bonaparte

Have you ever awakened from a nightmare twisted in the sweaty bedsheets only to see the rays of the benevolent sun pouring through the window and the bright blue sky telling you it is a new day and all is well? This is what the Fool now sees as he reaches the Sun card, and he rejoices that the long dark night of the soul has come to an end.

The Sun card may be the most simplistic card in the deck. Even dealt reversed it means good things to come, only on a lesser scale.

No matter what a client may have come to me to discuss, the appearance of the Sun card is a good omen. It is optimistic, positive, and a sign that all the best things will soon happen. But alas, this is not a concept that everyone can accept.

Let me introduce you to Rose, a longtime client and a lady who has a tremendous difficulty with happiness. Rose has had a hard life; she has battled and overcome abuse at the hands of her parents, an addiction to cocaine, and worst of all the devastating death of her only child, who at age thirteen fell off his bicycle, hit his head on a pavement curb, and died instantly.

What the cards tell me is that Rose's travails are behind her. The Sun always appears in her readings, but rather than greet this messenger with joy and a sigh of relief she immediately shuts down, eyeing the happy card with suspicion. Because she is so damaged from life, it is almost impossible for Rose to feel safe. Who can blame her? She'd better not let her guard down for a moment, because if she does she might again be surprised by a hideous situation. So she remains hypervigilant, which is an exhausting state to be in.

Another client I have is Pieter. Pieter is a hedonist, and although he is only thirty-five he looks like he is sixty. He burns the candle at both ends in a constant search for the ultimate high. He has flung himself out of planes wearing a parachute, climbed mountains, raced cars, and learned to walk barefoot on burning coals. Pieter also draws the Sun card often, and I notice that it seems to make him tense rather than happy. He interprets the card as a challenge that he can do more, testing the limits of his endurance. For Pieter the idea of happiness being found in a good book, in a blooming garden, or in quiet conversation with friends seems ridiculous, so he marches on toward bigger and better bangs.

Accepting joy is harder than it may seem. We look at people with great jobs, beautiful families, and winning lottery tickets and wish we were them. I have a client who won an enormous PowerBall jackpot and it almost ruined his life. For average people like you and me, listening to someone bitch about good fortune can be galling, but when good fortune is delivered at your doorstep unexpectedly, like every other major change in life, it requires a great deal of thought. If this were not the case, the Fool's path would end here, and the cards would say he lived happily ever after—but they don't. The Sun is just another way station in life, another lesson to be learned.

Happiness, like misery, forces us to make choices. Here is what happened to Paul the lottery winner. Like most of us he lived day-to-day with hopes and dreams of making his life a little better. He was not crazy about his job, but it paid the bills. He and his wife had a nice marriage, but over the years the thrill had diminished. When he played cards with his male friends, they tossed around fantasies of what they would do if they won millions of dollars. And then it happened to Paul, and it knocked him for a loop.

After winning an immense amount of money, Paul had an infinite number of choices to make, and making them was not fun the way he imagined it would be. He lived in a modest house in a middle-class neighborhood but now felt compelled to move to a mansion in the rich part of town. But he realized that all his friends still lived in the old neighborhood; he didn't know any of the wealthy folks who lived in the better part of town, and did not see fitting in with that crowd. Then he realized that the lottery money would also allow him to leave his wife and marry a gorgeous new one—a Playmate or even a Hollywood actress. But what would she expect him to do? Unlike his old wife she probably would not enjoy bowling or a meal out at the local diner.

Instead of commiserating with his friends about buying a new set of tires, the price of heating oil, and such, Paul was now approached by seemingly everyone he knew (and many he didn't) to lend them money. He knew he could quit his job, but what would he do with himself all day? His mailbox cascaded with heartbreaking letters from parents who could not afford a much-needed operation for their child, dogs and cats who should be rescued, starving children in Sudan, pensioners alone and frightened that they might become homeless if they missed rent, and a host of dreamers and schemers who all had inventions and projects that they wanted him to fund. Paul now found himself in a hell of happiness as he looked back nostalgically on the mundane joys of his old life.

Every day I am confronted with clients who can rejoice in the good things in life, but don't. I can tell you from years of reading tarot that there are some guidelines that seem to work and some that don't. First of all, don't confuse fantasy with reality. Using Paul as an example, learn to be comfortable with who you really are. Super-rich Paul was still at heart the Paul who clipped coupons and shopped at Wal-Mart. Paul realized that just because he could afford to did not mean he enjoyed constant travel or owning multiple houses in exotic parts of the world. He did not want to move away from his family and friends even if he had the money to. He was a man of simple tastes, back then as he is now. After much thought Paul built a very nice house in his old neighborhood, complete with a one-lane bowling alley. He stayed at his job, which was the last thing he ever imagined doing, but he found it gave him focus and a structure to his days. Without the stress of wondering how he would get along if he were ever fired, he enjoyed work. He hired an honest man to help him manage his wealth and made his best buddy into an assistant whose job it was to field the phone calls and sort through the mail so he did not feel over-whelmed. The friend was protective of him in a way no hired help could be, and it deepened their lifelong bond.

Paul funded his wife's dream of seeing the world, and because he didn't like to fly, he sent her off with her sister, first class, all the way around the globe. When she returned she was like a different person, and seeing her so bright and happy fanned the dying embers of their romance. He found that he loved to give her presents and surprises, and when he did it came from a sincere place in his heart. Paul successfully integrated his old life with his new fortune.

———•———

Do not fear the healing rays of the sun. As I write this, I think of poor Rose. When happiness tried to warm her world, she acted like a movie vampire and tried to hide in the darkness. Her attitude remained that if she was always sad and skepti-cal and had no hopes or dreams, she would be less dismayed when bad things happened. She tried to outfox fate this way. Rose imagined that to be sunny and optimistic was like wav-ing a red flag at a bull, that the gods of misery were watching her every mood and if she brightened they would squash her like a bug.

The funny thing is this type of behavior is collectively condoned by many Old World belief systems. Among Jews, Greeks, and Italians, to name but a few, it is standard practice that no one compliments anyone out loud or acknowledges accomplishments lest the good stuff be taken away. I had a friend who was confused and dismayed when not a single female relative of the ethnic family she had married into acknowledged the beauty or charm of her new baby. After asking around the community she lived in, she learned that the women did not want to endanger the baby by calling attention to its charms.

Rose did not integrate her past problems into her life well. She eventually drove away friends and even her long-suffering husband by being so miserably joyless. He had shared the loss of a son with her, but he did not want to have it front and center every second of every day as Rose chose to do. In Rose's mind, to not think about her boy was to not acknowledge that he had once lived. Thinking about him all the time kept him alive to her, but also left her alone. Not only could Rose not embrace happiness, she was terrified by it, so she lives in her proverbial dark cave hoping to attract no attention, comforted only by the company of ghosts from the past.

The last I heard from Pieter he was in a full-body cast at a hospital. He had jumped out of another small plane, but his chute had only partially opened. Had he not grabbed the hand of a fellow skydiver he would have been a splat on the sidewalk. As it is, he suffered great harm, breaking half the bones in his body. It was unclear if he would ever walk again or be wheelchair-bound for the rest of his life. When I spoke with him over the phone, I was surprised by his calmness. I had expected him to be jumping out of his skin (or his cast), and to tell me that he planned to soon climb Mount Everest in a wheelchair. I do not think it was the pain meds that made him sound so relaxed. It truly appeared that his enforced downtime had changed him. He seemed not depressed, but centered in a new way. Now that he was no longer chasing happiness, trying to cram every moment of his life with excitement, he finally became contemplative and focused. (I would say he now had time to smell the roses, but it turned out that Pieter was hideously allergic to flowers of all sorts, and when friends sent them to him at the hospital he sneezed so furiously that his broken body hurt like blazes.)

There is no one-size-fits-all answer when it comes to how to deal with happiness. People understand that sadness takes much getting used to and requires support from friends and relatives. What they do not realize is that happiness also takes much adjustment. Answered prayers, dreams coming true, or even enjoying one really good day may leave you feeling unequipped and guilty for these blessings. Needless to say Rose had the worst reaction of all to the promise of impending happiness. Being hypervigilant does not shield any of us from bad things happening any more than demanding happiness by shaking your fist at the sky will. Like the Fool we plod forward, making the best of each day and doing the best we can. That is all fate expects of us.

JUDGEMENT

JUDGEMENT

CARD NUMBER 20

A person will be called to account on Judgement Day for every permissible thing he might have enjoyed but did not.

—THE TALMUD

For some strange reason, as a tarot reader it took me a very long time to recognize the depth and drama of the Judgement card, even though it has all the elements that I, a Scorpio, love: big-time drama, gray-skinned dead people rising from their graves, and the apocalyptic sense of the end of times. Admittedly this card lacks the immediate cachet of Death or the Lovers card, but it is a huge and important Major Arcana card nonetheless. The Fool is winding down his journey. He has left the Sun with all its radiant happiness and contentment. Suddenly he is back on spooky, slippery ground. He is asked to admit and repent his wrongdoings. If I was the Fool at this point in my journey, I would whine,

"But I *did* that already." My panties would be in a knot and I would want to finish my tasks in life without being called on the carpet yet again to address my sins. This is getting tedious already!

Without a doubt the Fool has been called on over and over in his voyage to rid himself of his weaknesses and to edit the unnecessary from his life. So what is going on here?

The Judgement card has a different tone to it than previous cards where the Fool was asked to surrender his ego. For starters, this is the final judgement, where saints and sinners are separated, where the blessed rise to heaven and the others sink elsewhere. But I would add a twist to this card as well: If you've ever gone through the arduous process of psychotherapy, you may remember that when you hit upon a big revelation, it was closely followed by the realization that there was more work left to do. When therapy finally draws to an end, it is with the wisdom that no one is ever "cured," that even under the guidance of the world's best shrink you are and will continue to be a flawed person (we all are). But now instead of being ruled by your problems, you live comfortably among them.

For me the Judgement card is this mature view of ourselves as seen by the Fool. He is older, wiser, and not so "judgemental." Hopefully he has realized that people do the best they can with what they have, and in the greater scheme of things he is a lucky guy to have learned many hard lessons and survived. The Fool now understands that it is a smart man who can change his mind. He takes a position, but if the situation changes or he gains new knowledge, he may shift this position. He is no longer rigid in his beliefs, but flexible and understanding.

———•———

Here is a story about a client named Winnie. Winnie started out life with many friends. She was likable and pretty and had enough money to enjoy the finer things in life. She was easily folded into any crowd she wished to be a part of.

As Winnie got older, she became less fun to be with. She became sharp with her words and judgemental of everyone she met. I heard this when she told me her problems. She could not say anyone's name without adding a title. It was "that vile woman Anya," "that idiot boy Ronald," "Stephen, that addle-brained jerk." To be perfectly candid, at first this did not bother me; I found her salty tongue and un-saccharine comments amusing. After I knew her for a while, I realized that these names were never mentioned again. When I would ask, "What happened with Anya?" or another name previously spoken of, Winnie would sneer and say, "You could not possibly expect me to continue a friendship with someone like that!" Winnie went through people the way most of us do Kleenex—one quick use and then a toss into the wastebasket. It didn't take much time before I realized two things: She had run out of friends, and she wanted to see me all the time. I had become her paid companion who could not reject her because this was business. I also knew that if she had anyone left to talk to, eventually I would be known as "that charlatan Jane, who thinks she's so smart."

That is the problem with being very judgemental: You judge yourself into a very lonely place. I can say this with great feeling because being judgemental is one of my worst character flaws. For years I would draw an invisible line in the sand between me and friends, and if they stepped over it that was that. I would cut off people I had known for years for crimes and misdemeanors they never knew they committed. Would I tell them how they had offended me? Hell no, I was too self-righteous for that. Anyway they should have known! Like the Fool, age has tempered me, as I hope it will you.

What does this card mean dealt reversed? It can refer to the inability to make a decision, which is a way to stay stymied in your problems. It can also be about not wanting to face the music for whatever you have done that is wrong. When I was six years old I stole a ladybug pin from a millinery store in New York City where my mother went to buy her hats. When we got home she found the little pin, and I tearfully confessed that I had taken it. The very next day my mother and I rode a cab down to the store, where I gave the pin back to the store's owner and told him I had stolen it and was very sorry. Few things have left me with such a vivid memory. My mother could have ignored it or told me not to do it again, but that was not her style. Looking the man in the eye and telling him I was a thief was utterly awful. It was also utterly liberating, and I walked out of that store with this chapter closed and knew I would never live a life of crime.

My advice to you is that it is never too late to 'fess up to what you are ashamed of having done. Hold your own judgement day and clear the slate. There are a few ground rules:

Do not confess things to people that will hurt them possibly more than it hurts you to say them. Do you need to tell your husband you slept with his best friend if you are 100 percent certain that you will never do it again and he will never find out? I say suffer the guilt in silence to keep him safe from pain. It is also not nice to be so very truthful that you can't resist the urge to tell one friend that another friend said she looked fat, or that her husband had flirted with a neighbor. What is the point of this except to wound?

———•———

The Judgement card isn't just about admitting lies; it's also about confessing weaknesses. People barricade themselves so nobody can see their vulnerabilities, making them very confusing to be around. An example is a woman in my hometown whom everyone thinks of as an ice queen. She is always perfectly dressed and coiffed, her lip liner drawn with surgical precision. She never lets down her guard, never reveals anything about herself, and never offers an opinion. If you met her, you would think she was a snob and a frosty personality, while in fact she is wildly unsure of herself, afraid she is going to use the wrong word in a sentence, and terrified of letting people in on the fact that she grew up impoverished and uneducated. She has constructed such an impenetrable veneer that she lets virtually no one in to meet her real self. I often think the best thing that could happen to her would be to slip in a mud puddle in public and laugh at herself. She would endear herself to many people who now are afraid of her.

One final thought on being judgemental. A client of mine, Mindy, comes from a large, close family. She is in touch with them daily; they always visit one another and spend all holidays together. Mindy always makes a point of bragging to me how nonjudgemental her family is. The first thirty times I heard this I thought *How nice,* but after she incessantly repeated this I began to examine the situation. For Mindy, "nonjudgemental" was another way of saying that her family had no moral boundaries. They showed no difference in their treatment of family members who were college professors and family members who were sexual predators. One of the uncles was a prizewinning author, another a crack addict who repeatedly stole TVs to pay for his habit. It is nice to embrace your blood kin, but really, shouldn't the way people live their lives factor in just a little to how you judge them? I think the way Mindy's family acted was to take the easy way out and lump everyone into a big pile who shared the same last name. To blindly embrace people who are twisted, sick, or dangerous is strange. I am not talking about family quirks; everyone has a nutty relative or two (three, four, or five), and some relatives are more successful than others, some more fun to be around. But to me there is a big gap between blindly editing out the facts of someone's character to stay "nonjudgemental," and making a wise decision about whether this indeed is someone you want in your life.

The heart and soul of the Judgement card is not about passing that judgement on others, but allowing yourself to reveal your inner thoughts to yourself. It signals a time for deciding what works for you and what does not, who makes you feel good and who makes you feel like crap. Then, once you have figured out who you are in your inner mind, you must start the editing process and discard the people or things that no longer serve you well. Yes, this is selfish, but in a good way. Time is precious, and wasting it with those people or things you do not like or who do not like you is an insult to the universe.

I once saw in a novelty catalog a clock that ticks down all the seconds of your life. It estimates how long you will live, then shows you how much time you have left. I never bought the clock. I didn't think it was funny. With this clock in the room it would be impossible to watch a corny made-for-TV movie while stuffing your maw with popcorn, or take a long nap in the middle of the afternoon. Wasting time would not be an option, and I think we all need downtime. But watching this clock as you sit with people who make you unhappy, attend events that you hate, or stay at a job that is a dead end would make the ticking-down of your life a real signal to change your behavior. Every second of our lives is making us either better or worse. Please choose the former and not the latter.

THE WORLD

THE WORLD

CARD NUMBER 21

I don't believe in reincarnation, and I didn't believe in it when I was a hamster.

—SHANE RICHIE

Here is a World card story from my years as an EMT: A woman calls 911, and the ambulance responds quickly. The EMTs know she will not make it to the hospital before she delivers her baby, so they take her into the ambulance and prepare to help her deliver the baby then and there. As her contractions peak, she grabs one of the EMTs by the arm and squeezes as hard as she can. With a look of panicky determination on her face she declares, "I have changed my mind, I am *not* having this baby." A few minutes later the baby is born healthy; swaddled in a clean towel, he's placed on his mother's body as the ambulance makes its way to the hospital to finish the birthing process. The EMT who delivered the baby says, "I have seen many babies come out but I have never seen one go back up."

What, you may wonder, does this story have to do with the World tarot card? Pretty much everything. Some tarot books refer to this card as a woman or a man, and certainly both sexes have rebirth periods. But on the Rider-Waite version of this card you see a full-grown woman in the center of a womb-like ovoid shape made of braided leaves. This is an image not of the birth of an infant, but rather the rebirth of a female adult. The World card signifies a passage into another realm after much hard labor, and celebrates all we have gone through to get there. And as the panicky patient in the ambulance made us realize, once the process of birth or rebirth has started it does not reverse itself. If stopped in the middle, the result is a stillbirth, a very unhappy thing.

We all work hard to attain certain goals. We want a college degree, we want a good job, and we want secure love and a family. As we age we realize that these attainments do not fall into our laps without effort. We have to work for them; we "labor" away until we get to our goal. We fail only if we throw up our hands along the way and say, "I can't do this." Childbirth doesn't give us that option; the contractions move the baby forward into the world no matter how bad the pain is or how tired we are, or even if we loudly declare we have changed our minds. As they say about sharks . . . we must keep moving or we die.

As discussed, the World card shows a full-grown person being reborn—but is rebirth the beginning or the end of a stage of our life? The World card is the last of the Major Arcana cards in the deck, so it is appropriate that we question this image and its meaning. As an EMT I can tell you that, medically, birth is not the end of the pregnancy. That happens after the placenta is delivered. But arguably the birth of the actual baby and the cutting of the umbilical cord represent the end of a fetus's symbiotic life, and the production of a viable and separate human being who will thrive independently. Birth is an end, and birth is a beginning. Yes, that is what this card means.

The World card is the final stop on the Fool's journey from infancy to self-actualization. It signifies wholeness, a journey completed, and a heavenly ecstasy at the end of the path, where we are now one with the universe.

Of course the wisdom of the tarot is not about deciding on a name for your vacation home, but rather the big-ticket items like birth, death, and rebirth. Most of the world's religions share a concept of bodily death not being the end. Depending on whom you pray to, you will be reincarnated; be raptured up to heaven, where you'll enjoy the comfort of a slew of virgins; be a star in the night sky; be a ghost; burn in hell; or wait for eternity in a limbo purgatory that is even worse than the long lines at the Department of Motor Vehicles. In some way or another, most of us choose to believe that after we die we will still be around, because the prospect of nothingness is too uncomfortable and confusing to contemplate. The World card is tarot's way of saying, *Yes, you finish your life's journey but it is a joyful experience, and you get to start all over again.*

Now, what if your tarot spread includes the World card upside down (reversed)? That signifies an obstacle in completing your journey or goals. Imagine the annoying scenario in which you have worked extremely hard on something (a wedding, a job, a home being built), then suddenly, after you have dotted all your i's and crossed all your t's, everything comes to a grinding halt. Your mission doesn't fall apart; it just stops dead in its tracks. This is the World card reversed.

There could be a million reasons why this happens—the economy stinks, you fall out of love, important planets are in retrograde—but when things get bogged down and stuck, often there's little you can do but wait it out with grace and optimism. Unfortunately few of us do this; instead we sulk, lick our wounds, and withdraw into our shells. We blubber "Why, why, why" into our hankies, and do not understand how the bright future we so carefully planned is not happening. When the World card reversed hits the table, I am reminded of the army acronyms FUBAR and SNAFU. The world has punked you, and you do not like it one bit.

If we go back to the original metaphorical image of the World card as rebirth, a reversal means that your hopes and dreams are "stillborn," the forward movement has stopped in its tracks, and you are now sitting there with nothing happening. Stasis, lack of forward motion, is one of life's most painful situations. It takes so many different forms. Indecision, writer's block, procrastination, constipation, being on hold, sitting on a runway in a stalled plane, dithering around, forgetting obligations, not paying bills are all part of the same stalled behavior. Some of it is not your fault, some is. Obviously, to fix what you can is of prime importance. Apathy and indecision are all contrary to the promise of the World card.

———•———

This is the classic explanation of the World card, but in my readings I put my own spin on it. Often I get this card for (as the French say) women of a certain age. These ladies may be coming out of a life that is no longer satisfying. They are newly divorced, empty nesters, newly out of work, or experiencing some other major event. Rather than read this card as life's final chapter, I prefer to read it as a place somewhere between Act 2 and Act 3 in their lives. Act 1 has long been over; they are not young anymore, but neither are they old ladies. They are vibrant and smart and passionate midlifers, but they don't know what is ahead for them. As some people like to say, "No door closes without another one opening," and while this may be well and good it can be stifling and claustrophobic waiting in the hallway for said doors to open, close, and not whack you in the ass.

When I draw the World card reversed for clients, I explain it as an intermission that is nearly over. They have enjoyed Acts 1 and 2, and now—metaphorically—they are in the lobby having a glass of wine or a candy bar and getting ready for the curtain to rise on Act 3. It is not the end, but a transitional point in life that can be very frustrating and slow to resolve. It will, however, and it does.

Another traditional way to read this card is about traveling to a foreign land. Metaphorically I agree with this interpretation, as there is no foreign land more mysterious than our future.

There is no greater reward for a tarot card reader than seeing someone evolve. The hardest case I ever had was myself. I seldom read cards for myself; it's not a good idea, and readers rarely do it. While we can be clearheaded about other people's stuff, we tend to fly into frenzy when we confront our own issues. Because I do not read my own cards, and never read my husband's cards either, you can imagine how shocked and devastated I was when after almost forty years of marriage and a long professional career together he divorced me and quickly married another woman. Chronologically I was at the end of "Act 2," but it felt like the stage curtain had come crashing down on my head. Because my marriage had been for me the defining thing in my life, to suddenly be alone was incomprehensible. I could not imagine a future; I could not imagine making it through the day.

But the wisdom of the World card had other plans for me. I felt like the lady in the ambulance declaring that she would *not* have the baby. I dug in my heels, refused to believe what was really happening, and said no to everything. How could I be single, how could I be alone, how could I balance my checkbook, how could I pay bills? I cried until I had no tears left. I tried to analyze the situation and found no plausible answers. What was I to do with myself?

It is now two years since my divorce. What I focused on at the start of this whole mess was getting a new husband. I now realize that this could wait; what I needed even more was a new me.

I bought a small cottage and painted it yellow and blue, *my* favorite colors, not my ex-husband's. I got rid of almost all my old possessions and used the money to buy new girl-friendly furniture. Shabby chic white linen couches replaced brown leather; a tiny crystal chandelier in the kitchen makes me smile, as does a whimsical four-poster bed with a polka-dot ruffle. Instead of making my new house a lair for a new man, I made it a nest for the current me. It is a soft place to land, a house that as soon as I walk into it makes me feel whole instead of half.

I changed my conception of friendship as well. When I used to see ladies having lunch or jogging together, I often thought, *Poor things, they don't have a man.* My girlfriends up until this point had been people I would see only when I was not busy with my husband. My lady friends were and still are there for me in a way so deep and meaningful, I can hardly describe it. They all said the same thing: "Call me anytime night or day if you need to talk." They check in with me, they have the key to my house, they know what medications I take if I get sick; they even send my French bulldogs birthday cards. So maybe my worst fear came true: I am an older lady living alone with ugly little dogs, and you know what? I kind of like it. In my wildest dreams I never thought I could get through the agonies of this "rebirth." More than once I shut down, unable to move on. When I sold my "married" house, which I loved for a very long time, I lived in a motel for the summer while I was trying to find a place to live. Now settled in my own place, I have confronted getting ill by myself, my furnace breaking down in the middle of winter, the computer crashing, my car being dead in the driveway, my checkbook not balancing, and a hundred other disasters of life to which my first reaction had always been to call my husband and have him fix it.

So I too have been reborn, and it hurts and it is a visceral and difficult process. But as they say: "What's the alternative?" I could have cried the rest of my life, but I ran out of tears. I could have kept my girlfriends at arm's length, but they were the salve for my wound. This period in my life has also made me a far better tarot reader than I was before. If compassion, empathy, hope, and love are the cornerstones of the human condition, then I have a good foundation with which to help people. I had to find these things on my own terms, and hopefully I can help others on their path as well.

A Note to the Reader

I encourage you to try reading the tarot, or having it read for you. Use it correctly and you will be rewarded tenfold. The deck is a magical entity that somehow does tap into the subconscious and give us answers. Never use the cards with malice, do not push them into areas they do not wish to go, and do not set yourself up as being better than your clients. Even the most talented readers are human and subject to being humbled by life.

About the Author

Jane Stern is well known for her food writing and her weekly contribution to PRI's *The Splendid Table*. She is an emergency medical technician whose memoir *Ambulance Girl* was made into a movie starring Kathy Bates as Jane.

Before any of these successful careers, Jane was reading tarot cards, a skill she learned from her mother and grandmother. Her great-grandmother was a spiritual healer who traveled through rural Russia on horseback.

She began reading tarot cards professionally over forty years ago, and in the last decade has lectured and taught classes on tarot.

She lives in Ridgefield, Connecticut, with her two French bulldogs, Elmer and Cecil.

Her website is janemastertarot@yahoo.com, or she can be reached for an appointment at (203) 438-4028.